ALEXANDER ARCHIPENKO
A Centennial Tribute

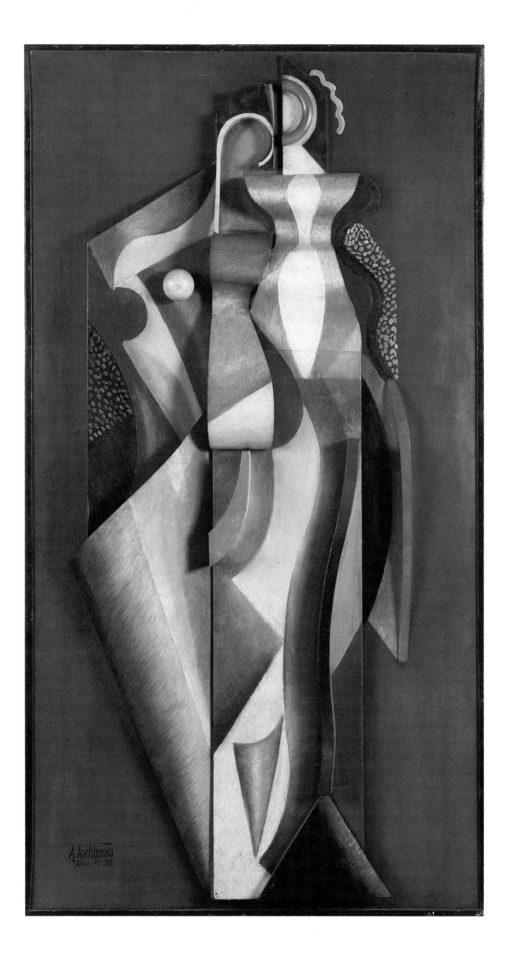

ALEXANDER ARCHIPENKO
A Centennial Tribute

Katherine Jánszky Michaelsen
Nehama Guralnik

National Gallery of Art
Washington

The Tel Aviv Museum
Tel Aviv

EXHIBITION DATES
National Gallery of Art, Washington
16 November 1986–16 February 1987

The Tel Aviv Museum, Tel Aviv
12 March–13 June 1987

This catalogue was produced by the Editors Office, National Gallery of Art, Washington. The type is Electra, set by Composition Systems Inc., Falls Church, Virginia. Printed by Eastern Press, Inc., New Haven, Connecticut, on Vintage Velvet paper.

Edited by Jill B. Steinberg
Designed by Phyllis Hecht

Distributed to the trade by
Universe Books
381 Park Avenue South
New York, N.Y. 10016
ISBN 0-87663-510-9

The exhibition is supported by an indemnity from the Federal Council on the Arts and Humanities.

COVER: *Woman at Her Toilet*, Alexander Archipenko, The Tel Aviv Museum, Tel Aviv (cat. no. 24)

FRONTISPIECE: *Two Women*, Alexander Archipenko, National Museum, Belgrade (cat. no. 32)

Library of Congress Cataloging-in-Publication Data
Michaelsen, Katherine Jánszky, 1944–
   Alexander Archipenko, a centennial tribute.

Catalog of an exhibition held at the National Gallery of Art, Washington, Nov. 16, 1986–Feb. 16, 1987 and at the Tel Aviv Museum, Mar. 12–June 13, 1987.
1. Archipenko, Alexander, 1887–1964—Exhibitions.
2. Archipenko, Alexander, 1887–1964—Criticism and interpretation. I. Guralnik, Nehama. II. Archipenko, Alexander, 1887–1964. III. National Gallery of Art (U.S.) IV. Muse'on Tel Aviv. V. Title. VI. Title: Alexander Archipenko.
NB237.A7A4   1986   730'.92'4   86-18118
ISBN 0-89468-096-X

CONTENTS

FOREWORD

THE NATIONAL GALLERY OF ART and The Tel Aviv Museum are
pleased to be jointly organizing and exhibiting *Alexander Archipenko: A
Centennial Tribute*. For the first time, Archipenko's important early
work has been brought together with his significant later sculpture; the
show encompasses nearly six decades of sustained artistic production.

Archipenko was his most creative when living in France from 1908 to
1920, and in Paris he undertook a series of innovations that ultimately
have established him as a pioneer of twentieth-century sculpture. He
worked with untraditional materials such as glass, sheet metal, found
objects, and mirror, as well as plaster and bronze. A contemporary witness to the cubist style of Picasso, Braque, and Gris, he took up many of
their concerns, exploring concave and convex forms and experimenting
with negative space. Archipenko invented the void, and his insistence
on its importance gave a new shape, literally and figuratively, to sculpture. He also introduced rich color into his constructions, engaging in
our century's first consistent exploration of the possibilities arising from
a fusion of painting and sculpture. Bold modeling in space is frequently
combined with intricate, painted trompe l'oeil effects. The resulting
polychromed constructions, called "sculpto-paintings" by their maker,
are Archipenko's seminal contribution to modern sculpture.

The current exhibition is the product of generous cooperation. The
Tel Aviv Museum has loaned important early pieces from the Erich
Goeritz Collection, works which have not circulated since Goeritz sent
them to Tel Aviv in the 1930s. Later sculpture, from the artist's estate,
has come to the show from his widow, Frances Archipenko Gray. We
are immensely grateful to these and all the other lenders who have generously consented to share their rare constructions with a broad public.
In addition, we appreciate greatly the indemnity granted the exhibition
by the Federal Council on the Arts and Humanities.

The project was coordinated at the National Gallery by Jack Cowart,
curator of twentieth-century art, with guest curator Katherine Jánszky
Michaelsen, and at The Tel Aviv Museum by Nehama Guralnik, curator of European and American art. We are indebted to Dr. Michaelsen
and Ms. Guralnik for the essays they have contributed to this catalogue,
which also contains color illustrations of the polychromed pieces and is

Alexander Archipenko, *Carrousel Pierrot*, 1913 (see page 27).

the most specific scholarly reference devoted to Archipenko's full career of sculpto-paintings and hand-formed painted constructions. It is our hope that the exhibition and the catalogue will provide important opportunities for assessing Archipenko's crucial role in the development of twentieth-century art.

J. CARTER BROWN
Director
National Gallery of Art

MARC SCHEPS
Director
The Tel Aviv Museum

Lenders to the Exhibition

Eric and Salome Estorick

Frances Archipenko Gray

The Solomon R. Guggenheim Museum, New York

Hirshhorn Museum and Sculpture Garden, Smithsonian Institution

Donald Karshan Collection, Florida

Moderna Museet, Stockholm

The Museum of Modern Art, New York

National Museum, Belgrade

Perls Galleries, New York

Philadelphia Museum of Art

Private Collections

The Tel Aviv Museum

Yale University Art Gallery

Note to the Reader

Titles   In the text and entries, alternate titles for Archipenko's works are given in parentheses

Dates   Dates not in parentheses are inscribed dates; dates with parentheses are assigned dates.

Dimensions   Dimensions are in order of height, width, and depth, and are given in inches, followed by centimeters in parentheses

Abbreviations   NGA   National Gallery of Art, Washington
TAM   The Tel Aviv Museum

Notes   After the first full reference to a source, all subsequent citations are abbreviated with author, date, and page number

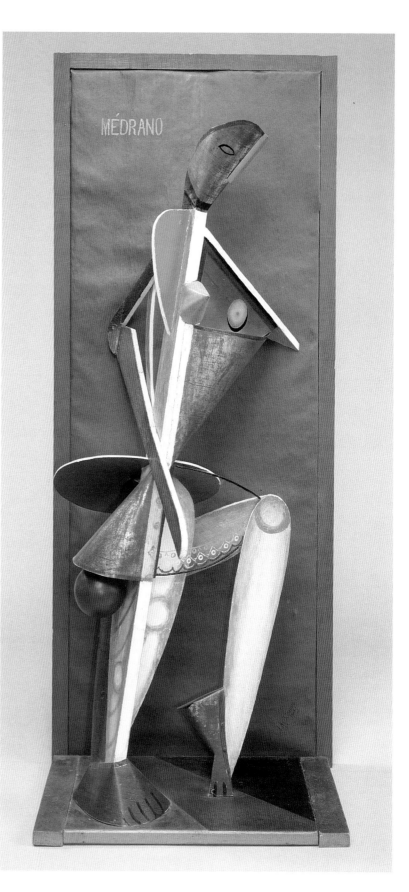

Alexander Archipenko, *Médrano II (Dancer)*,
1913 (see page 27).

Alexander Archipenko, *Bather*, 1915 (see page 39).

CHRONOLOGY

1887   Born 30 May, in Kiev, Ukraine

1902–1905   Studied painting and sculpture in Kiev art school.

1906   Went to Moscow, worked and participated in group shows.

1908   Left for Paris at age 21. Frequented La Ruche, the artists' colony.

1910   Began exhibiting in the Salon des Indépendants with the cubists (showed again in 1911, 1912, 1913, 1914, and 1920).

1911   Exhibited in the Salon d'Automne with the cubists (also in 1912, 1913, and 1919).

1912   Exhibited at Moderne Kunst Kring, Musée Municipal Suasso, Amsterdam (6 October–7 November) and at La Section d'Or, Galerie La Boétie, Paris (10–30 October). Joint exhibition with Le Fauconnier at Museum Folkwang, Hagen, Germany (7 December–8 January 1913). Opened art school in Paris.

1913   Represented by four sculptures in the Armory Show, New York. One-man exhibition, Der Sturm Gallery, Berlin (September); included in *Erster Deutscher Herbstsalon*, Berlin (20 September–1 November) and in *International Post-Impressionist Exhibition*, Budapest.

1914   Participated in a large international cubist exhibition at the Mánes Fine Arts Association, Prague (February–March). *Médrano II*, a mixed-media construction, caused a sensation in the Salon des Indépendants. Represented in the *Esposizione Libera Futurista Internazionale*, Rome (13 April–25 May); in the Third International Exhibition of De Onafhankelijken, Amsterdam (May–June); and in the Salon des Artistes Indépendants, Brussels (16 May–7 June). Began to make sculpto-paintings.

1914–1918   Spent war years in Nice.

1917   Publication in Berlin of *Alexander Archipenko—Sturm Bilderbuch II*.

1919   Participated in a large group exhibition at Galerie d'Art des Editions Georges Crès & Cie., Paris (27 May–14 June). One-man exhibition, Librarie Kundig, Geneva (24 November–10 December) and Kunsthaus Zürich (8 January–8 February 1920).

1920   Represented in La Section d'Or exhibitions in Paris (Galerie La Boétie), Rotterdam, The Hague, and Amsterdam. One-man exhibition in the Venice Biennale (15 April–31 October). Exhibited twenty works in the *Exposition Internationale d'Art Moderne*, Geneva (26 December–25 January 1921).

1921   One-man exhibition, at the Société Anonyme, Inc., New York (1 February–15 March). Tour exhibition in Germany (Berlin, Dresden, Wiesbaden, Hannover, and Munich); retrospective exhibition, Potsdam. Moved to Berlin; opened art school. Married Angelica Schmitz (Gela Forster), a sculptor. Publication of monograph *Archipenko Album*, with texts by Theodor Däubler and Iwan Goll (Potsdam).

1922   Joint exhibition with Lyonel Feininger at Kunstsalon Ludwig Schames, Frankfurt. Participated in *Erste Russische Kunstausstellung*, Galerie van Diemen, Berlin.

1923   Represented in the *Exhibition of Russian Painting and Sculpture*, Brooklyn Museum, New York (23 January–4 March). One-man exhibition at Publicace Devetsilu, Prague (April–May). Moved to the United States (arrived 16 October); opened art school. Publication of four monographs in Europe (Maurice Raynal, Erich Wiese, Ljubomir Micić, and Hans Hildebrandt).

1924   One-man exhibition, Kingore Gallery, under the auspices of the Société Anonyme, Inc. (20 January–4 February). Started summer art school, Woodstock, New York. Publication of expanded version of *Alexander Archipenko—Sturm Bilderbuch II*, with text by Roland Schacht (Berlin).

1927   Patents issued for *Archipentura* (Apparatus for Displaying Changeable Pictures and Method for Decorating Changeable Display Apparatus, nos. 1,626,496 and 1,626,497) on 26 April. Tour exhibition (Denver, Los Angeles, San Diego, Oakland, and Portland).

1928   One-man exhibition, Anderson Galleries, New York (October).

1929   Became an American citizen (6 May). Bought thirteen acres near Woodstock, New York; began construction of complex of buildings for art school and studio. Established Arko, a laboratory school of ceramics in New York.

1932   Lectured in colleges and universities on Pacific Coast, in the Midwest, and the East.

1935	Took up residence in Los Angeles and opened art school.
1935–1936	Taught summer sessions at the University of Washington, Seattle. Represented by six sculptures in Alfred Barr's exhibition, *Cubism and Abstract Art*, at the Museum of Modern Art, New York.
1937	Moved to Chicago and opened art school. Joined the faculty of the New Bauhaus (headed modeling workshop).
1938	Returned to New York; reopened art school and summer school in Woodstock, New York.
1944	Exhibition of works from 1909 to 1944 at Nierendorf Gallery, New York (18 January–5 February). Taught at Dalton School, New York.
1946–1947	Returned to Chicago; taught at the Institute of Design.
1947	Began making carved plastic sculpture with illumination.
1950	Taught at the University of Missouri, Kansas City.
1950–1951	Lecture tour of southern cities of the United States.
1951	Taught at Carmel Institute of Art, California, the University of Oregon, and the University of Washington, Seattle.
1952	Taught at the University of Delaware, Newark. Exhibition of drawings, Museu de Arte Moderna, São Paulo, Brazil.
1953	Elected Associate Member of International Institute of Arts and Letters. Exhibition of drawings, El Instituto Guatemalteco, Guatemala City.
1954	Large retrospective exhibition, Associated American Artists Galleries, New York (16 October–14 November).
1955–1956	Tour of one-man exhibition in Germany (Düsseldorf, Darmstadt, Mannheim, Recklinghausen).
1956	Taught at University of British Columbia, Vancouver, Canada.
1957	Exhibition of recent polychrome works and sculpto-paintings at Perls Galleries, New York (further exhibitions in 1959 and 1962). Angelica Archipenko died at age 65 (5 December).
1959	Awarded gold medal, XIII Biennale d'Arte Triveneta, III Concorso Internazionale del Bronzetto, Padua, Italy (October).
1960	Published *Archipenko, Fifty Creative Years, 1908–1958*, by Alexander Archipenko and Fifty Art Historians (New York). Married Frances Gray, a sculptor and former student (1 August). Recovered a group of early plasters stored since 1921 by friends in Cannes. Traveling exhibition in Germany (Hagen, Münster, and Düsseldorf).

Alexander Archipenko, *Woman with Fan*, after first stage of restoration, 1981 (see page 129).

1962	Retrospective exhibition, Winnipeg Art Gallery, Canada. Exhibition, Galerie Wilhelm Grosshennig, Düsseldorf. Elected to the Department of Art of the National Institute of Arts and Letters.
1962–1963	Exhibition, Galerie "Im Erker," St. Gallen, Switzerland (17 November–10 January 1963).
1963	Exhibitions in Milan (Centro Culturale S. Fedele) and Rome (Ente Premi Roma).
1964	Exhibition, Galerie Stangl, Munich (14 February–4 April). Died 25 February, in New York.
1967	Traveling memorial exhibition sponsored by the UCLA Art Galleries.
1969	Traveling exhibition, International Art Program, Smithsonian Institution, Washington.
1970	*Archipenko: The Parisian Years*, Museum of Modern Art, New York (20 July–18 October). *Archipenko: The American Years, 1923–1963*, Bernard Danenberg Galleries, New York (23 July–15 August).
1973	Exhibition, Pace Gallery, New York (22 September–20 October).
1974	Exhibition, Fuji Television Gallery, Tokyo (5–24 April).
1976	Exhibition, Zabriskie Gallery, New York (also in 1979 and 1982).
1981	*Archipenko, The Early Works: 1910–1921*, Tel Aviv Museum, Israel (April–September).
1985	*Archipenko: Sculpture, Drawings, and Prints, 1908–1963*, Norton Center, Danville, Kentucky (23 March–6 May). *Archipenko: Drawings, Reliefs and Constructions*, Edith C. Blum Institute, Bard College, Annandale-on-Hudson, N. Y. (24 August–26 October).

KATHERINE JÁNSZKY MICHAELSEN

KATHERINE JÁNSZKY MICHAELSEN

Alexander Archipenko
1887–1964

When a specific temperament interlocks with a favorable position the fortunate individual can extract from the situation a wealth of previously unimagined possibilities.

George Kubler, *The Shape of Time*, 1962

I.

ALEXANDER ARCHIPENKO (Aleksandr Porfirevich Arkhipenko, 1887–1964) left his native land in 1908. The decade that followed his arrival in Paris was his most creative and original period. In the stimulating artistic atmosphere of Paris in the heyday of cubism, Archipenko made a number of important innovations in sculpture. By 1921 he had exhibited widely throughout Europe and America. When he was thirty-three he was honored with a retrospective at the Venice Biennale, which was at the time the most prestigious art event in the world. Hailed by critics and art historians for his revolutionary approach to form, materials, and color, he was considered by many to be the greatest living sculptor. In 1923 Archipenko left Europe for the United States and his career suffered an eclipse. He continued to make sculpture, had numerous exhibitions, and taught and lectured all over the country, but when he died in 1964 his fame still rested largely on the brief, intensely creative interlude fifty years earlier.

Two months before his death in February 1964, Alexander Archipenko broadly summarized his life and work for the French periodical *XXe Siècle*.[1] At the time of this final interview, the often retold tales had coalesced into a kind of personal mythology. The interview is revealing not for its factual content, most of which had already entered the literature, but for the image it projects. It begins and ends with Archipenko's credo: the artist's most precious faculty is invention. He linked this idea to his father, an inventor and engineer who had made a fortune with a furnace designed to purify noxious factory fumes. Because Archipenko decided to be an artist rather than an engineer like his father, the relationship between the two was permanently strained. Yet, all his life Archipenko restlessly pursued "invention," somewhat in his father's sense of the word. He spoke of his innovations in sculpture as "inventions," and following his father's example, even made forays into the field of mechanical design.

As an art student Archipenko describes himself as a rebel: he was expelled from art school in Kiev, where he was born, because he and his friends opposed its academic conservatism; in Moscow he belonged to a small group of progressive artists who held exhibitions together; and in Paris he left the Ecole des Beaux-Arts in disgust after only two weeks. Archipenko recalls that he began making sculpture in 1904. While still at art school in Kiev, he received his first commission from a wealthy Polish landowner. After making the sculpture for his patron, Archipenko took the opportunity of staging a small exhibition in a store in the neighboring village. This being 1905, the year of the first Russian revolution, his first visitor was a police officer who demanded to know why the sign at the entrance stated that admission for workers and peasants was cheaper, and pointing to a painted sculpture titled *The Thinker*, asked what he was thinking about and why he was painted red. Archipenko remembers having great trouble convincing the police officer that it was merely a technical experiment and that no symbolism was attached to the color. This incident, as recounted by the artist, illustrates both his political liberalism and the precocity of his innovative use of color in sculpture.

Another discovery that was very significant for his future work is said to have been made during his childhood in Kiev. Archipenko remembers his parents bringing home two identical vases. He said that as he looked at them, he was seized by the urge to place them close to each other. No sooner had he done this, he discovered a third, immaterial vase formed by the space between the first two. Archipenko later saw this experience as the basis for his theory of the void as "symbol" for an absent volume.

One of Archipenko's earliest memories of sculpture, as described in the interview, was of a statue in the gardens of the university in Kiev where his father worked. It was a simple stone idol measuring about five feet in height. Archipenko explained that it was made before sculpture was banned with the advent of Christianity in the Ukraine in the ninth century. He vividly recalled how awed he had been by this mysterious ancient image, whose impact subsequently influenced his taste in art. Years later, at the Louvre, he was unmoved by great masterpieces like the *Mona Lisa* or the *Venus de Milo*, and concentrated instead on Byzantine, Gothic, and archaic art. During visits to the Trocadéro (ethnographic museum) he noted similarities between the primitive and folk arts from diverse regions of the world. He recalled once seeing a wooden plate with what looked like a design from his native Ukraine only to find that it came from Oceania. Years later in the United States he discovered that the art of the American Northwest in some ways resembled African art. In the context of his broad eclectic approach to sources, Archipenko made a statement to his interviewer in 1963 that can be considered a paradigm for his entire career:

What Plato says about ideas is true, they are in the air. One can get them everywhere. That is why one finds the same things, similar religions, similar works of art in very distant places. In short, everything exists in the universe. Come, take it if you can.

Archipenko left Russia in 1908. When he arrived in Paris, he attached himself to that city's artistic vanguard, the artists and critics who would become future advocates of cubism. He made many acquaintances at La Ruche, the artists' colony in the Vaugirard district. He met Léger, with whom he became close friends and with whom he exchanged works. (When short of cash they would entertain in the streets, Archipenko singing Russian songs to Léger's accompaniment on the harp.) At La Ruche, Archipenko also met Apollinaire, Cendrars, and Raynal; all three, especially Apollinaire, were instrumental in the development and propagation of cubism, and by writing about Archipenko they played an important role in his career. Through Léger, Archipenko also came into contact with Delaunay, Le Fauconnier, Gleizes, and Metzinger. By 1911 Archipenko was part of the group that had formed around the Duchamp brothers (Jacques Villon, Raymond Duchamp-Villon, and Marcel Duchamp), and he attended their Sunday meetings together with Gleizes, Léger, Le Fauconnier, Metzinger, Gris, Lhote, Picabia, and others. In addition, there were cubist gatherings in the studios of Le Fauconnier and Gleizes.[2]

When in 1910 the cubist painters first exhibited as a group at the Salon des Indépendants, Archipenko and Duchamp-Villon were also included as "cubist" sculptors. Although sculptors were present among the ranks of the cubist painters from the very start, their works lacked specific cubist features until about 1912. Also, the inclusion of Archipenko and Duchamp-Villon had more to do with their personal friendships than with any actual cubist style present in their sculpture. In 1910 and 1911, by creating simpler, generalized forms, they were merely reacting to the over-modeled surfaces of the "impressionist" sculpture of

Rodin and Medardo Rosso.

The 1910 Salon des Indépendants was both the first manifestation of cubism in general, as well as Archipenko's first public showing in Paris. He exhibited five sculptures and one painting. Four of the sculpted works were of nudes in idyllic landscapes. The figures, either alone or in groups of two or three, are engaged in ritual actions that recall the work of Gauguin. *Sorrow* (*Tristesse*), 1909 (cat. no. 1), for example, is a very small painted wood sculpture that is rectangular in shape. It shows a female figure standing on top of a boxlike base decorated in front with a head flanked by upraised arms in the manner of an early Christian *orant*. The squared-off head of the figure is completely bent over one shoulder, and the enlarged hands are raised to the face in a ceremonial gesture. The vegetation next to the figure is of an imaginary and tropical kind with large fruits. The wood is painted greenish-brown with a naive artist's exaggerated concern for details like eyes, lips, fingers, nails, and toes.

The square shape and melancholy gravity of *Tristesse* point ahead to a group of blocklike figures in stone and marble made in 1910/1911. *Mother and Child*, 1910–1911 (cat. no. 3), for example, was exhibited in Brussels in 1911 at the Salon des Indépendants. (Archipenko was among the selection of artists from France that included Delaunay, Ségonzac, Le Fauconnier, and Léger. Apollinaire described them all as cubists in the preface to the catalogue.) The solid marble block contains mother and child, the infant clinging to its mother like a baby koala. Both are massive, with greatly enlarged flat hands and feet. Stylized linear incisions describe the details of face and body. The image is basic and powerful, and generally archaic in feeling. These qualities are also evident in the wood and stone sculpture of Picasso, Derain, and Brancusi from the years 1907 and 1908, but the presence of these qualities may also reflect Archipenko's response to what he saw on his frequent visits to the Trocadéro and the Louvre.[3]

Archaizing and primitivizing were preludes to cubism in painting as well as in sculpture (for example, Picasso was indebted to African and Iberian art). In their search for alternatives to impressionism, painters and sculptors alike employed these "primitive" sources to arrive at the new vocabulary of clear massive forms that became the point of departure for cubism. With a new emphasis on formal and structural problems in sculpture, subject matter began to lose the importance it had in the late nineteenth century, as is demonstrated by the many generically titled works by Archipenko and others. The female figure or bather often became a pretext for experiments in plastic form.

Concerning the stylistic developments in sculpture, when asked in

Fig. 1. Alexander Archipenko, *Bather*, 1912, cast stone, 40½ (102.5) h. with base, Museum Bellerive, Zürich.

1923 about his youthful response to Rodin during the early years in Paris, Archipenko was blunt: "I hated Rodin, who was then fashionable. His sculptures reminded me of chewed bread that one spits on a base, or of the crooked corpses from Pompeii."[4] With this statement, Archipenko focuses on two aspects of Rodin's art that the new generation of sculptors disliked: the elaborate surface modeling and the use of emotionally charged subject matter. Despite their criticism of Rodin, the sculptors of Archipenko's generation owed him a great debt. One of his most important contributions was to show that a figural fragment could be a complete work of art. Following Rodin's example, Archipenko began in 1910/1911 to take great liberties with the human form, chopping off arms and legs at will. Unlike Rodin, however, whose partial figures were the result of a process of editing and condensing, Archipenko conceived his figures as partial from the very start.[5] *Bather* (fig. 1) and *Porteuse* (cat. no. 6), both of 1912, are examples of this increasingly reductive approach to the human body. Both have one arm cut off level with the breast, the other cut just above the hand. In *Porteuse* the legs end just above the knees, while those of *Bather* are cropped just below the knees.

Bather is a big piece. The total height of approximately forty inches, base included, is about double that of *Porteuse*, an average-sized work for this sculptor throughout his career. *Bather* stands in an exaggerated contrapposto; the upper and lower portions of the torso twist in opposite directions creating a spiral movement that invites the viewer to move around the figure, which is very well conceived from all points of view. The body parts are simplified and devoid of details. The thighs are flattened out and the greatly projecting right hip forms a sharp angle that is repeated in reverse by the position of the head. The thickened neck is unified with the head in a shape that echoes the left shoulder stump. The absent arm is not missed; on the contrary, the curtailing of this limb is necessary to maintain the balance of the sculptural mass. Nor is the truncation of the legs disturbing; the bather's left leg sinks into the base as into water, while the other absent leg is daintily lifted "out of the water."

The lunging female figure with a wrestler's shoulders is aptly titled *Porteuse*, meaning "carrier" or "bearer." It is among a small number of female figures by Archipenko that are defiantly unfeminine. The hips are level and the separated legs suggest a lumbering forward motion. The body is composed of faceted, angular forms that are repeated: head, breasts, and left shoulder stump are similar in shape. The outsized right shoulder, in turn, recalls the shape of the thighs. Three parallel horizontal grooves mark groin, waist, and neckline. This analytical approach to

the human figure and the reduction of its parts to simplified, repeated forms are signs of an incipient cubism.

The forward-bending curve of *Porteuse* is an idea Archipenko had been experimenting with for a couple of years. It is first seen in a lost work, *Salome*, of 1910. Further trials were made in 1912/1913 in other lost works such as *Venus* and *Red Dance* (fig. 2), finally culminating in *Leaning Woman (Penché)*, 1913–1914 (cat. no. 13), which far surpasses the others with its greatly arched form. The head projects far beyond the edge of the base, which is widened at the bottom to counter the threat of imbalance. A triangular bracket supports the tapered footing. *Leaning Woman* can be viewed as a radically abstracted and reduced version of *Porteuse.*

The projecting shoulder stump in *Bather* and *Porteuse*—a frequent feature of Archipenko's partial figures—is resolved in the elegant, streamlined *Flat Torso*, first conceived in 1914. The piece exists in a variety of different mediums and finishes which Archipenko fabricated over the years to satisfy a steady demand for replicas of this popular work (cat. no. 18). The elongated legs, cut below the knees, swell gracefully at the thighs, and the hip and upper torso form a right-angled zig-zag. A diagonal slash eliminates one shoulder and breast entirely; the other breast is sliced off in the middle. From the side, *Flat Torso* is an undulating sliver; from the back it is geometrically severe—the buttocks form a straight horizontal ridge that meets the line separating the two legs to make a rigid T-shape. *Flat Torso* is the type of figure most commonly identified today with Archipenko: a female torso with a flowing arabesque contour. Repeatedly throughout his career, Archipenko returned to this universally pleasing motif. Whether vertical or horizontal, or merely suggested by an S-shaped outline, the curvilinear female torso is the formal *idée fixe* in Archipenko's work.

Fig. 3. Alexander Archipenko, *Seated Woman* (1911), plaster, c. 22 (56) h., location unknown.

More specific cubist features begin to appear in Archipenko's sculptures of the years 1911 and 1912. The first of these is an angular fragmentation of planes that derives from similar effects in cubist painting, where faceting is the result of the analysis of solid forms. In *Seated Woman (Draped)*, 1911 (fig. 3)—a lost plaster that was remade by the artist in the 1950s and cast in bronze—the drapery covering the figure consists of sharp-edged flat segments; in *Madonna of the Rocks*, 1912 (cat. no. 7), also a plaster, the base is a fanciful arrangement of interlocking angular parts that no doubt inspired the Leonardesque title.[6]

Surface fragmentation in sculpture is, of course, prefigured in Picasso's *Woman's Head* of 1909 and in Matisse's *Back I* and *Back II*, dated 1909 and 1913, where the human form is analyzed and recreated by means of flat circumscribed parts that meet at sharp angles. Archipenko, however, does not fragment the bodies in *Seated Woman (Draped)* and *Madonna of the Rocks*. Other than cropping one arm, he leaves the anatomies intact. The women have monumental legs and bulbous breasts and knees. The somewhat overwrought quality of these sculptures results from the obvious contrast between their rotund swollen forms and the cool geometric planes that surround them.

An unexpected and striking feature of *Madonna of the Rocks* is its color—a uniform paprika-red covers the entire work. (With time it has acquired a beautiful patina.) Because the various elements—mother, infant, rocky setting—are not differentiated, the color undermines the representational character of the work. It transforms the sculpture into an object, independent of what it claims to represent. This is analogous to Picasso's famous *Still Life with Chair Caning*, 1912 (Musée Picasso, Paris), where, because the work is oval-shaped and has an unusual rope frame, it must be regarded not only as a representation of something but as an object in its own right.

Although the two principal cubists, Picasso and Braque, did not take part in the activities of the other cubist artists (they lived somewhat removed in Montmartre and exhibited only privately in galleries), there was some contact between them. Delaunay and Metzinger met Picasso, and Léger knew both Picasso and Braque.[7] There is no record of meetings between Archipenko and either Picasso or Braque, but he was able to keep abreast of their innovations through friends and from visits to the Kahnweiler Gallery, where there was always a selection of their works.[8]

In 1912/1913 Picasso and Braque began to make collages. By pasting scraps of paper and pieces of cloth on the canvas, they affirmed the flatness of the two-dimensional surface and rejected the spatial illusionism of traditional perspective. The switch from brush-and-paint to scissors-and-paper precipitated a change in style; instead of breaking up a painted form into numerous parts each carefully colored and shaded, with the new technique the artist was able to create larger, simplified, coherent substitutes for forms.

Archipenko quickly adopted the new medium of collage in a series of remarkable figure studies made in 1913. In two that are titled *Figure in Movement* and *Figure* (cat. nos. 8 and 9), he reduced the human form to six or seven cut-paper shapes that are pasted down and unified by a few deft strokes of the pencil or crayon. Because he was a sculptor thinking in plastic terms, he shaded the flat paper shapes to suggest the volumes of sculpture. Archipenko used the lessons learned from making two-dimensional collages in his three-dimensional sculpture. The result was a departure from the unified, continuous massing of traditional sculpture to a disjunctive assembly of separate parts. The first conclusive example of this important development is Archipenko's *Geometric Statuette*, 1914 (cat. no. 16). Like a collage, it consists of clear-cut components with distinct junctures and a clear overlapping of forms that spell out the step-by-step process by which the work appears to have been assembled.

Along with the influence of cubist collage, *Geometric Statuette* displays an element borrowed from cubist painting—the optical ambiguity achieved by pairing concave and convex forms. One of the concepts of cubism is that solid and void are of equal value and can interpenetrate and even substitute one another. In cubist painting, the transposition of concave and convex forms began to appear in Picasso's and Braque's

Fig. 4. Alexander Archipenko, *Woman Combing Her Hair* (1915), bronze, 13¾ (35) h., Collection, The Museum of Modern Art, New York, Acquired through the Lillie P. Bliss Bequest.

Fig. 5. Alexander Archipenko, *Walking Woman* (1918–1919), terra-cotta, c. 27 (68.5) h., location unknown.

paintings of 1908 and 1909. Umberto Boccioni (1882–1916), the Italian futurist, transferred these spatial ambiguities to sculpture in 1912, and there is a tentative early example of this principle in the spherical projections and depressions on the base of Archipenko's *Madonna of the Rocks*, 1912. The large scooped-out shape next to the protruding right buttock is a deliberate cubist counterpoint.

By 1914, Archipenko began to interchange concave and convex forms in his sculpture. This was made possible by optical illusion—under certain lighting conditions, receding forms appear to protrude and protruding ones appear to recede. This happens because shadows which surround a rounded shape are also formed inside the edges of a hollow. The incorporation of the effects of light into the design of the sculpture was an important innovation. As Albert Elsen has written, "Where for centuries artists had worked to free their figure sculptures from the effects of optical distortion, Picasso and Archipenko made them their collaborator and the 'accidents of light' became a controlled part of craft."[9]

While it exemplifies the new manipulation of mass and void, *Geometric Statuette* is perhaps most important because it is the first known instance of the innovation that was later to be singled out as Archipenko's major claim to fame—the hole. In this piece, the concave form of the head is deeply gouged out to create an opening in the back. As the final stage in the hollowing-out process of a concavity, the void paradoxically becomes the substitute for its absolute reverse—the mass of the head. The hole is not only one of the principal features of cubist sculpture but a significant step in the development of sculpture in general; it signals the opening-up of the traditional monolithic concept of sculpture. (Later works by Archipenko in which the hole is found are: *Statuette*, 1915 [cat. no. 19], *Woman Combing Her Hair*, 1915 [fig. 4], *Walking Woman*, 1918–1919 [fig. 5], and *Seated Woman*, 1920 [cat. no. 29].)

Archipenko's innovation was termed *Lochplastik* ("sculpture of holes") in Germany in the 1920s and touted as a major discovery. In the inflated prose characteristic of the time, Iwan Goll writes:

Archipenko is the first to dare what appears to be sculptural suicide. A deep philosophy emanates from his creations. Every object is also present in its reverse. Being and non-being. Fullness is expressed through emptiness. A concave form is inevitably also a convex form. . . . Archipenko's discovery—to stress the presence of something through its absence—makes even the unimaginable possible.[10]

Archipenko's introduction of the void as a positive element in sculpture continues to be regarded as one of his significant contributions. George Heard Hamilton writes:

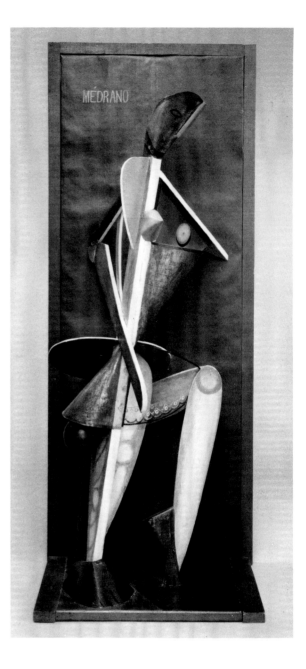

Fig. 6. Alexander Archipenko, *Carrousel Pierrot*, 1913, painted plaster, 23⅝ (60) h., Collection, The Solomon R. Guggenheim Museum, New York. (Illustrated in color page 7.)

Right: Fig. 7. Alexander Archipenko, *Médrano II (Dancer)*, 1913, painted tin, wood, glass, and painted oilcloth, 50 (127) h., Collection, The Solomon R. Guggenheim Museum, New York. (Illustrated in color page 10.)

Archipenko's use of concave and convex volumes within the same figure, and his discovery of the volumetric significance of the void, were important contributions to modern art.[11]

Archipenko later realized the importance generally attributed to his innovation and devoted an entire chapter in his 1960 book to "Modelling of Space."[12] Disregarding the traditional belief that "sculpture begins where material touches space," he concluded (in 1912) that "sculpture may begin where space is encircled by material." In this context he cites the Chinese philosopher Lao-Tze (sixth century B.C.) and Henri Bergson (1859–1941), in whose writing he found confirmation of his ideas. He quotes the following passage from Bergson's *Creative Evolution* (1907):

. . . object once annihilated, leaves its place unoccupied; for by hypothesis it is a *place*, that is a void limited by precise outline, or, in other words, a kind of a *thing*.

Believing that "in art the shape of the empty space should be no less important than the meaning of the shape of solid matter," Archipenko writes that he developed a "symbolic" use of space in which "by its absence the object leaves its own form in our memory."

The hole was an important feature in the works of other artists after Archipenko. For Lipchitz, the hole, as seen in *Man with a Guitar*, 1916 (stone, The Museum of Modern Art, New York), for example, emphasizes the three-dimensionality of the figure; it forces the viewer to move around the sculpture and helps assert its reality as an object.[13] For Henry Moore, who has acknowledged Archipenko's influence in this regard, the hole is a device that relates the opposite sides of a sculpture to each other.[14]

Whatever the meaning or the function ascribed to the hole, it was an important breakthrough that, as noted earlier, had its origins in cubist painting. Archipenko's timely association with the cubists helped him achieve special recognition early in his career. He was only twenty-five when, in 1912, he was given the opportunity to show a large selection of his sculpture at the Museum Folkwang in Hagen, Germany in a joint exhibition with Le Fauconnier.[15] Archipenko found his first patron and collector in Karl-Ernst Osthaus, founder of the museum. In 1913 his works were seen in two distant points of the world: at the Armory Show in New York and in Budapest.[16] Patronage by Herwarth Walden of Der Sturm also began in 1913, with Archipenko's first one-man show in Berlin. From then on, Archipenko's sculpture and drawings were frequently reproduced in the influential monthly *Der Sturm*, and he regularly participated in group exhibitions organized by Walden. In 1917 the second volume of the *Sturm Bilderbücher* series was devoted entirely to Archipenko's work.

Fig. 8. Alexander Archipenko, *Gondolier*, 1914 (reconstructed c. 1950; enlarged and cast, 1957), painted bronze, 72⅛ (181) h., Hirshhorn Museum and Sculpture Garden, Smithsonian Institution, Washington.

The year 1914 may well have been Archipenko's greatest. At the Salon des Indépendants that spring the four sculptures he showed—*Carrousel Pierrot*, 1913 (fig. 6), *Boxing*, 1914 (cat. no. 14), *Médrano II*, 1913 (fig. 7), and *Gondolier*, 1914 (fig. 8)—are among his most important and widely discussed works. Although since 1911 Apollinaire had been giv-

Fig. 9. *L'Intransigeant*, Paris, 2 March 1914, pages 1 and 2.

ing Archipenko brief but positive notices, during the 1914 exhibition his support became enthusiastic. In response to a sarcastic review by one of his colleagues at *L'Intransigeant*, Apollinaire came forcefully to Archipenko's defense. His 2 March column (fig. 9) devotes an entire paragraph (the longest commentary) to Archipenko:

Rooms 11 and 9. Here is where one can see Archipenko's sculptures. One of them is made of different materials—glass, zinc, wood—all polychromed. It represents a very great effort to go beyond the conventional in sculpture. Those of my colleagues who are so certain they possess the ultimate truth in aesthetics have, of course, the right not to mention such a surprising work, executed with such ease and grace. As for me, I am happy to say how delighted I was at the sight of such a delicate work. The other polychrome statuette exhibited in the middle of Room 9 is no less interesting, and I really pity anyone who remains indifferent to the charm and elegance of Archipenko's gondolier, a slender black statue exhibited in Room 11.

Soon afterward, in part because his editors openly sided with the other critic, Apollinaire resigned from the newspaper.[17]

In his admiration for Archipenko's entries in the 1914 Salon, Apollinaire was not alone. Alberto Magnelli (1888–1971), the Italian painter and supporter of futurism, actually purchased three works. While the cost involved could not have been considerable, Magnelli's decision to buy three of Archipenko's sculptures attests to the high esteem in which the Italian futurists held the young artist. *Carrousel Pierrot*, *Boxing*, and *Médrano II* remained in Magnelli's collection until they were sold to the Guggenheim Museum in New York in the mid-1950s. Archipenko was well known in Italian avant-garde circles. Boccioni is said to have visited his studio in 1912;[18] and the futurists invited him to send works to their *Esposizione Libera Futurista Internazionale*, which was being held that same spring in Rome.

Amusement park, boxing ring, circus tent, and Venice are the settings of the four pieces Archipenko exhibited in the spring of 1914. The presence of significant content—direct references to contemporary life, with its color, movement, and light—is rare for this artist, whose customary subject at the time was the nude generically titled "Bather," "Woman," or "Statuette." The success of these four works (none of which, incidentally, contains the Archipenko trademark of the curvilinear female torso) may be due to the lively subject matter.

"*Venez rire*" ("come and laugh") is the inscribed invitation that greets the viewer as he approaches *Carrousel Pierrot*, a composite of figural and mechanical elements skillfully fused in a *Mensch-Maschine* ("man-machine"). This term was used by Iwan Goll in his 1921 essay; he reports that the idea for the piece came to Archipenko on the occasion of the feast of Saint Jacques when "dozens of carousels with horses, swings, gondolas and airplanes imitate the rotation of the earth."[19] The two diagonals that rise from the base, the flaring cone, the disc, and the ball on top can be read as the legs, upper torso, wide ruffled collar, and head of Pierrot, the clown. The lateral projections—a ball on one side and a cigar-shaped element on the other—may signify arms. At the

Fig. 10. Raymond Duchamp-Villon, *The Horse*, 1914, bronze (cast c. 1930–1931), 40 (101.6) h., Collection, The Museum of Modern Art, New York, Van Gogh Purchase Fund.

same time, the bright colors and the smooth, machined forms evoke the mechanical merry-go-round: the large oblique disc is now read as the top of the structure from which hang various objects, the "horses, swings, gondolas and airplanes" of Goll's description. The implied rotating movement and the fusion of man and mechanical object in *Carrousel Pierrot* are examples of concepts important in both cubism and futurism—simultaneity and the machine aesthetic. Both concepts were also adopted by Duchamp-Villon and can be seen in his sculpture *The Horse*, 1914 (fig. 10). Ideas about simultaneity, transition, and change were derived in part from the philosophy of Bergson, whose *Creative Evolution* had a strong effect on the members of the Puteaux group.[20]

Carrousel Pierrot is a panoply of color—red, green, blue, and black, as well as pink, light blue, orange, and cream. In keeping with the sense of a carnival, the colors seem to have been chosen by impulse and arranged spontaneously. Contrasting bands of color produce a feeling of rotation: as one moves around the work, it seems itself to move; each step is punctuated by a change in color. The multicolored wedges of the "torso," for example, cause the eye to travel in a circular path; the division of the "head" into uneven segments of red, black, and white gives the illusion of spinning motion. The carefree, improvised character of the color belies the complex composition.

Archipenko explored the dynamic relationship between sculpture and the space it occupies and surrounds in a series of paired figures, most notably, *The Dance*, 1912–1913 (fig. 11), a lost work which exists in later bronze versions in two sizes. In this piece the two dancers serve merely as a frame that encloses a large central space. One seated, the other standing, the figures touch only at the point where their hands meet, forming an archway. In addition, because the figures have their legs set wide apart, they enclose space in depth as well. This three-dimensional orientation is also found in *Carrousel Pierrot*, where the crosslike element in the front extends horizontally, vertically, and backward; from the central axis two spokes—one blue, one pink—branch off and curve back. This arc is continued by the cigar-shaped "arm" of Pierrot and forms a frame around a large space visible from the side. To conceive of sculpture in this way, as a framing device for space, with space not only taking an active role, but, one might say, becoming the very reason for the sculpture, was unprecedented, and the importance of this development was noted by many contemporary writers.[21]

A superb collage in the collection of the Moderna Museet in Stockholm that Archipenko made in 1913 (*Collage: Two Figures*, cat. no. 10) explores the problem of space in the two-dimensional medium. The pieces of bright red paper that make up the two interlocked figures are

pasted onto a dark gray-green background, creating an intricate and dynamic play between figure and ground. Painted white highlights, black shadows, overlapping, and foreshortening (left leg of the figure in front) suggest depth and volume, while several manila-yellow boomerang shapes schematically trace the movement of the figures.

A firsthand account of Archipenko during these years was given by the Hungarian sculptor Béni Ferenczy (1890–1967).[22] Although written late in his life and ostensibly somewhat negative in its bias, it provides a rare glimpse into Archipenko's early creative period in Paris. After a first visit in 1911, when he attended the studio of Bourdelle, Ferenczy returned to Paris in 1912/1913 and tried various sculpture schools before coming to Archipenko's. The school, which advertised carving in hard materials, was recommended to him by an ex-student of Matisse. Ferenczy had had some carving experience and reports scornfully that the sandstone the three Russian students at the school were working with seemed very soft to him. He describes a Portuguese plaster caster in Archipenko's studio, a fat mustachioed monarchist, with

31

whom he became friendly. He was an excellent craftsman who patiently polished Archipenko's plaster sculpture with the finest powders until they were very shiny. On one occasion Archipenko is said to have told Ferenczy that although he seemed talented, his aesthetic ideals were outmoded and that he should not insist on working in an old-fashioned style like cubism!

One major event Ferenczy remembers was a lecture on modern sculpture that Apollinaire presented at the school. The studio was emptied and benches and chairs were brought in. On the appointed evening the dimly lit room filled up slowly. Apollinaire arrived and sat down at a table with a petroleum lamp. Ferenczy describes an imposing figure, tall and strong, fair-skinned, blond, in a black suit and bow tie. Apollinaire spoke in a ringing tenor voice and what he said outraged Ferenczy. In his opinion, Appollinaire's utterings about the superiority of archaic over classical Greek sculpture, the Italians' lack of talent in sculpture and their destruction of European taste in the sixteenth century, were only meant to shock the audience. The final insult, in Ferenczy's eyes, was Apollinaire's declaration that until the appearance of Archipenko, the only true sculptors had been the Negroes of Africa. Ferenczy points out that Picasso, Derain, and Vlaminck were not present at the lecture, nor were the important dealers. Of the better-known artists only Marie Laurencin (who, according to Ferenczy, was Archipenko's mistress at the time) had attended. For Ferenczy, Apollinaire's speech could only be explained as outright propaganda intended to promote sales for Archipenko because he had very few buyers and was always forced to ask his students to advance their monthly twenty franc tuition fee.

In his recollection of his Paris sojourn, Ferenczy dwells at some length on the subject of boxing. Professional boxing had been introduced in France a few years before and was a favorite topic of conversation among artists in cafés. The prizefights attracted large crowds, and Ferenczy reports that when a French boxer beat a foreigner the spectators would break out singing the *Marseillaise*. Ferenczy describes with relish the appearance and exploits of the fighters, most of whom were black, and vividly recalls seeing Joe Jeanette, the half-black, half-Indian, French heavyweight champion at a café on the boulevard des Italiens.

Two black forms locked in combat is the subject of Archipenko's most famous sculpture, *Boxing* (cat. no. 14). Although the work verges on the abstract, the idea of physical struggle is evident immediately: two pointed triangular shapes are the heads and torsos of the fighters with their cone-shaped arms driving into each other. The deadlock seen in the frontal view dissolves as one walks around the piece, which exhibits a variety of dynamic silhouettes with the forms twisting, arching, and punching into the space around them.

Without minimizing Boccioni's impact—visible in the dynamic forms and implicit movement of Archipenko's *Boxing* and Duchamp-Villon's *The Horse*, for example—it is important to keep in mind that there was a great mutual interest and fruitful exchange of ideas between the Italian futurists and the artists working in Paris. Since the publication of Marinetti's literary manifesto in *Le Figaro* in 1909, futurist ideas were very much a part of the Parisian artistic climate. For the futurists the fundamental elements of the modern world were motion and speed, elements they sought to incorporate in their art. Cubism, which Carrà and Boccioni encountered in Paris in 1911, provided the futurists with a formal language that they adapted to express simultaneously the various phases of continuous motion. Boccioni was keenly interested in developments in Paris and kept himself informed through frequent visits and correspondence with friends who lived there.[23] In 1912, the year he published his futurist sculpture manifesto, he visited the French capital three times. On one of these trips he concentrated exclusively on sculpture, visiting the studios of the avant-garde sculptors of the time—Brancusi, Duchamp-Villon, and Archipenko.[24] In June 1913 he held his *First Futurist Exhibition of Sculpture* at the Galerie La Boétie in Paris. His innovations, as summarized by Apollinaire in a review, were "varied materials, sculptural simultaneity, violent movement."[25]

Between 1912 and 1915 a number of artists—notably Boccioni, Tatlin, Puni, Baranoff-Rossiné, Laurens, Lipchitz, and Archipenko—began to experiment with constructing sculpture out of various materials.[26] Early in 1912 Picasso extended the cubist analysis of forms into real space with his first relief construction out of sheet metal and wire.[27] A few months later Braque created the first collage: adding scraps of paper and cloth to the cubist canvas, he introduced to painting the process of construction and the mixing of media. Both steps had significant repercussions in the development of sculpture. With these new materials mass in sculpture is achieved in a new way. Instead of being replicated as in traditional sculpture, forms are schematically outlined; planes joining and intersecting in space create a conceptualized model of mass.

Archipenko may have been the first sculptor fully to take on the challenge of the new aesthetic. He gave 1912 as the year when he began working with different materials,[28] and this is his date for *Médrano I*, his first multimedia construction (fig. 12); the earliest documented date for this lost work, however, is spring 1914.[29] Subtitled *Juggler*, it was named after the Cirque Médrano, a favorite haunt of many Paris artists. Even if dated 1913–1914, Archipenko went way beyond his cubist contempora-

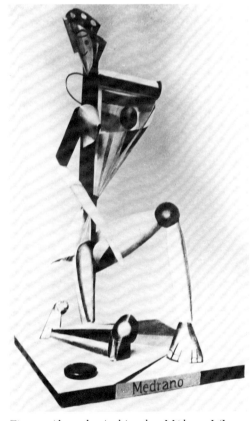

Fig. 12. Alexander Archipenko, *Médrano I (Juggler)* (1912–1914), painted wood, glass, sheet metal, and wire, c. 38 (96.5) h., location unknown.

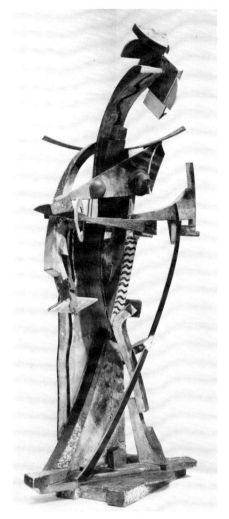

Fig. 13. Vladimir Baranoff-Rossiné, *Symphony Number 1* (1913), polychromed wood, cardboard, and crushed eggshells, 63¼ (161.1) h., Collection, The Museum of Modern Art, New York, Katia Granoff Fund.

ries: instead of creating a small relief, he made a freestanding work that was over three feet tall; instead of showing still-life objects, he assembled parts to represent the human figure; instead of using only one or two materials, Archipenko combined wood, sheet metal, wire, and glass.

Médrano I had another novel feature—it incorporated movement, both real and implied. The diagonal arm was actually movable, and the spherical forms elsewhere in the composition imply movement. According to Archipenko's notes, the spheres of the knees and the breast were also meant to be understood as the juggling balls tossed by the circus performer.[30]

Médrano II, subtitled *Dancer*, was the sensation of the 1914 Salon. On 28 February Apollinaire wrote in *L'Intransigeant:*

The most innovative and most graceful exhibit, in my opinion, is Archipenko's: polychrome sculptures in various materials. Glass, wood and tin are here combined in the most novel and successful way.[31]

On 2 March, the day after the official opening of the Salon, the front page of *L'Intransigeant* carried an illustration of *Médrano II* with the following caption:

We reproduce here the photograph of the work of art (?) praised elsewhere in this issue by our collaborator Guillaume Apollinaire, who assumes sole responsibility for his opinion.

Apollinaire had also singled out, in his review of 28 February, "the very important polychrome work by M. Rossiné . . . ." Vladimir Baranoff-Rossiné (1888–1942), also known as Daniel Rossiné, was a painter whose known sculptural work consists of three freestanding constructions.[32] The piece mentioned by Apollinaire was *La Symphonie*, a complicated structure of folded sheet-metal forms that is known today only from a photograph. (Deeply embittered by the mockery with which the press received his work, Rossiné is said to have thrown it into the Seine.) A surviving early mixed-media construction by him is *Symphony Number 1*, 1913, at the Museum of Modern Art, New York (fig. 13).

It is no wonder that Baranoff-Rossiné's and Archipenko's constructions caused a furor in 1914. They challenged the accepted notion of sculpture at its very roots. Instead of marble, bronze, or the familiar plaster, these new works were made of mundane substances like wood, glass, metal, and wire. Instead of being carved or modeled—two respected crafts whose mastery was itself considered an achievement—they were nailed, pasted, and tied together with no apparent attempt to hide the junctures, seams, or nails. And in startling contrast to the generally monochromatic sculpture of the time, these works were painted in bright contrasting colors.

Unlike Archipenko's first construction, *Médrano II* is not completely freestanding: the figure is attached to a back panel in three places. The backdrop provides support while it helps to control the outline and clarify the composition. The major subdivisions of the body—head, shoulders, torso, hips, and legs—are clearly stated. A brightly-colored 1913 collage, *Composition* (cat. no. 11) employs a similar vocabulary of separate oval and triangular shapes united by linear elements. In *Médrano II* flat planes branch out into space from a central shaft that extends from top to bottom. The shoulders are made up of a semicircular blue plane that intersects with another oblique plane. The hips are represented by a larger, inclined, circular green plane, which fans out at the rear. Yet another plane, a wedge-shaped piece of glass with a lace pattern painted on the border, represents the dancer's transparent costume. A cone-shaped piece of folded sheet metal completes the hip.

The description of volume by means of articulated planes would later constitute the essence of Naum Gabo's space-revealing sculpture. Between 1912 and 1914 Gabo is known to have visited Paris, where his brother Antoine Pevsner had been living for some time. Pevsner brought him into contact with the cubists and may have introduced him to Archipenko, an old acquaintance from Kiev. Stimulated by what he had seen in Paris (which included Archipenko's work at the Salon des Indépendants), Gabo made his first constructed sculptures out of small intersecting planes of wood, opaque plastic, or sheet iron in 1915 in Norway, where he and Pevsner spent the war years (for example, *Constructed Head No. 1*, 1915, fig. 14).[33] (Archipenko's use of glass in *Médrano II* predates Gabo's and Pevsner's work with transparent materials which began in 1920.)

Color in *Médrano II* articulates structure and isolates the various materials. The dominant tone is the rich, opaque red of the backdrop, against which the bright, sharp-edged forms are distinctly set off. A different shade of red appears in the nose, breast, and arm, and it is mixed with white to create a pink flesh tone for the legs (one is illusionistically modeled, the other is painted to suggest the bone structure underneath). Three colored sections on the base symbolize cast shadows. A bright white is used for the main structural elements—the slightly inclined central shaft and the shorter oblique shaft on the right. White edges on the blue and green planes of the shoulders and the hips stress their flatness and clearly describe their shapes. Red bands border all the cone-shaped, unpainted metal parts that represent the face, upper torso, lower torso, and feet.

Fig. 14. Naum Gabo, *Constructed Head No. 1* (1915), plywood, 21 (53.5) h., © Graham and Nina Williams, 1986 (photo c. 1922).

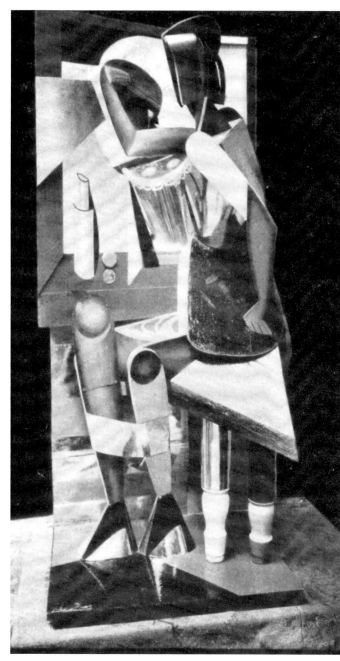

Top left: Fig. 15. Alexander Archipenko, *Woman in Front of Mirror* (1914), glass, wood, metal, and mirror, c. 6 ft. (180) h. (destroyed).

Top right: Fig. 16. Alexander Archipenko, *Head* (c. 1957), bronze, 15 (38) h., Courtesy Zabriskie Gallery, New York.

Fig. 17. Henri Laurens, *Clown*, 1915, painted wood, 20¾ (53) h., Moderna Museet, Stockholm.

Fig. 18. Jacques Lipchitz, *Detachable Figure (Seated Musician)* (1915), painted wood, 19¾ (50.2) h., Yulla Lipchitz Collection.

Clarity and logic of structure and composition distinguish *Médrano II* from the constructions of Archipenko's Russian colleagues. In Rossiné's *Symphony Number 1*, for example, the pieces (some of them ready-made furniture parts) are assembled in a humorous and haphazard fashion to form a figure. But Rossiné paid scant attention to anatomical truth, and the title itself, with its reference to music, is nonfigurative. The outline is erratic and aggressive. Color is applied in a random fashion with the whimsical inclusion of crushed eggshells at the base. *Médrano II*, however, with its traditional circus theme, is clearly representational. It has an even and balanced outline, the tilted hips of the dancer suggesting a contrapposto position, and the use of color is purposeful and systematic. Despite its unconventional materials and novel technique, when compared to *Symphony Number 1*, Archipenko's construction can well be termed classical.

The visual ambiguities of cubist painting, particularly the intricate spatial compositions of some of Gris' still lifes, are closely paralleled in another large, full-figure construction Archipenko made in 1914. *Woman in Front of Mirror* (fig. 15) was illustrated in Apollinaire's periodical *Les Soirées de Paris* in June 1914, appeared in exhibitions in 1920 and 1921, and was then lost or destroyed.

Woman in Front of Mirror, a six- to seven-foot high construction, had a base and backdrop like *Médrano II* and showed a woman seated on a triangular stool in front of a dressing table with a real mirror in which her head and torso were reflected. Archipenko's notes indicate that a still life and the woman's right arm were painted *on* the mirror.[34] In addition to wood, glass, and mirror, shiny metal foil was used to cover part of the base, the woman's feet, one of the legs of the stool, and the lower part of the backdrop. The presence of these highly reflective materials prompted Raynal's observation that "Archipenko no longer sought to sculpt forms, but to sculpt light itself."[35] A bronze head (fig. 16), based on the head in *Woman in Front of Mirror*, was dated 1913 by Archipenko but was made much later, in the 1950s;[36] it shows a head composed of intersecting planes that describe volumes similar to those in *Médrano II*.

Henri Laurens and Jacques Lipchitz began making freestanding constructions a little later. Examples are *Clown*, 1915 (fig. 17), by Laurens and *Detachable Figure (Seated Musician)*, 1915 (fig. 18), by Lipchitz. They are smaller than *Médrano II*, and both are made only of wood. The forms used to construct the body in the Laurens piece—the pointed, triangular upper torso and the round, inclined plane of the hips—may have been inspired by the similar arrangement in Archipenko's controversial construction of the year before. In the work by Lip-

Fig. 19. Alexander Archipenko, *Bather*, 1915, oil and pencil on metal and wood and paper, 20 x 11½ (50.8 x 29.2), Philadelphia Museum of Art, The Louise and Walter Arensberg Collection. (Illustrated in color page 11.)

chitz, the grooved neck and the head sprouting dried leaves are African-looking, while the painted shirt front recalls Elie Nadelman's contemporaneous and widely discussed figures with painted clothing. All three constructions are mock serious puppets that evoke popular culture and street life—the ambiance of French cubism.

In August 1914 Germany declared war against Russia and France. With the advent of World War I the international community of artists living and working in Paris was disrupted. In 1915 Marcel Duchamp lamented in New York:

Paris is like a deserted mansion. Her lights are out. One's friends are all away at the front. Or else they have already been killed.[37]

Archipenko left Paris; he did not return to Russia, as did most of his compatriots, but chose to sit out the war in the south of France. "Also living in Nice," reported Apollinaire in March 1915, "is the sculptor Archipenko, whose wife sends sweaters to their friends in the French army."[38]

In Nice, where he lacked the studio facilities and materials required for traditional sculpture techniques, Archipenko occupied himself predominantly with sculpto-painting. He described this as "a panel uniting colors and forms . . . interdependencies of relief, concave or perforated forms, colors and textures . . . made of papier-mâché, glass, wood or metal . . ."[39] The freestanding constructions of before had been troublesome to make, the product unwieldy and fragile. Thus, like other artists, Archipenko abandoned this type of sculpture for the more enduring sculpto-painting, where the various materials are firmly attached to a rigid back panel and project only modestly into space. Between 1914, the documented date of the first known sculpto-painting (*Woman with Fan*, 1914, cat. no. 17), and the early 1920s, Archipenko made close to forty sculpto-paintings of which only about half have survived. Also belonging to the category of sculpto-painting are some painted, freestanding, modeled pieces in papier-mâché, terra-cotta, or plaster (cat. nos. 23 and 30).

The significance of the sculpto-painting in Archipenko's work has thus far not been fully recognized. Known primarily from black and white reproductions and often dismissed as a hybrid form,[40] the sculpto-paintings may well constitute Archipenko's most original body of work. It is precisely the unexpected passage from one medium to the next—from projecting volume to pictorial surface—that is the unique quality of the sculpto-painting. Although in subject matter and style they rely on cubist paintings, the compositions are conceived with a greater spontaneity and imagination; they are entirely free of aesthetic constraints. The most striking feature of the sculpto-painting is dazzling, dissonant color. Unfortunately, both the peculiar coloristic effects and the quirky shifts from relief to flat painted surface are virtually lost in reproductions. The present opportunity of viewing a dozen early sculpto-paintings gathered together for the first time (in the current climate that favors eclecticism and shuns dogma) may finally rescue these works from the neglect they have long suffered.

In an essay printed in a German exhibition catalogue (1922), Archipenko refers to sculpto-painting as his most important work. He explains:

Take for example the sculpto-painting *Bather* [1915, fig. no. 19]. Here I rendered the shape of a figure stepping out of the water with a column nearby. The form is yellow, the water blue. How absurd it would have been if I had attempted to carve the color of the water and the color of the figure. Naturally I have to paint. I have tried representing a form that does not have color and I

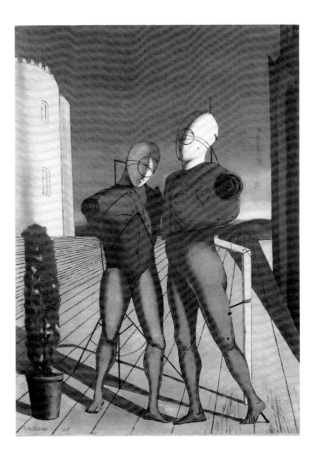

have found none. Do you know a form that has shape and that does not at the same time have color? For me sculpto-painting is not only something logical, but it is absolute truth. If I were a Futurist I would say that every sculpture in bronze, marble, wood, that any sculpture in a single material, is a lie.[41]

In addition to the unity of form and color in sculpto-painting, Archipenko also stressed the importance of the presence of actual shadows (those cast by the relief elements) and the possibility of varying the shadow effects by moving the light source.[42] By combining painting and sculpture, Archipenko created a new medium of representation.

The figure in *Bather* is composed of flattened metal cones placed end to end. The upper cone contains the head, chest, and one arm raised above the head. A small spherical form attached to the cone represents the breast; the other breast, in profile, is painted in. From the second arm, a cylindrical form, hangs a painted grayish-white towel. The rest of the picture is drawn in pencil or painted and locked in place by a few major compositional lines. One line rises diagonally from the base of the column at the left to meet the adjoining side of the two metal cones. Another line, slightly to the right of the first, cuts through the lower metal cone, creates the form of a thigh, and continues beyond the figure to meet the dark painted frame on the right. The cone of the upper torso is part of a larger segment of a circle whose arc echoes the curve of the arm raised above the head. These arbitrary compositional lines that work with, against, or independently of the subject, are strongly reminiscent of the distorted perspective lines and sharply delineated areas of shadows in Giorgio de Chirico's paintings (for example, fig. 20). Given Archipenko's contacts with Italian artists, it is likely that he was aware of de Chirico, who was in Paris between 1911 and 1915 and exhibited in the Salons.[43] (The classical column at the left in *Bather* may be a direct quote from de Chirico's work.) In addition, on a more profound level, the disquieting stepping in and out of reality in Archipenko's sculpto-paintings, that is, from relief (reality) to painting (illusion), parallels the eerie coexistence of reality and dream in de Chirico's metaphysical landscapes. In *Bather* a bright orange color suffuses the entire small panel. The only areas that escape the unreal golden glow are the dark, painted frame, the brilliant wedges of blue water, and some green and red highlights. The color transports the mundane bather into a mysterious otherworldly realm.

Another work evoking a sense of mystery is the brilliantly colored panel titled *Before the Mirror (In the Boudoir)* of 1915 (cat. no. 20). This astonishing precursor to Picasso's famous 1932 painting of the same subject shows both the woman and her ghostly green reflection within the frame of a mirror situated behind a dressing table. The two images—one yellow, one green—not only occupy the same space but are inextricably mingled. A yellow arm comes out of a green shoulder, and green arms extend from the yellow body. The yellow body is painted and flat but has a projecting relief head; a pink chest and breast in relief protrude from the painted green reflection. Shiny sheet metal covers the unoccupied portions of the mirror, which is framed on two sides by a rust-red color.

This prescient little picture has an interesting still life in the foreground. A blue flask half filled with a yellow liquid is set against a background of patterned paper and casts a blue shadow on a green field; the neck of the flask overlaps the edge of the frame and is transformed into a shadowy reflection. A yellow, painted picture frame contains an actual photograph of a dapper Archipenko in a hat. (This predates by several years the dadaists' first use of photographs in their work of c. 1919–1920.)[44] In addition, the display of brightly colored and precisely outlined geometric shapes that completes the still life prefigures the postwar style of Léger and other purist artists like Ozenfant and Jeanneret (Le Corbusier).

In subject matter, *Woman with Fan II* (cat. no. 21) and *In the Café* (cat. no. 22), both of 1915, fall within the customary repertory of cubism. These works may lack significant content, but they are rich in formalist invention. *In the Café* is a collage of three or four superimposed flat layers of wood. Except for the slanted table top which projects slightly into space, the other relief elements (chest, fan, carved table leg, and the band on top of the head) remain close to the picture plane. Visual puns abound: breasts are represented by flat round cutouts; relief cup and saucer cast a painted shadow on the table top; and flat painted areas are illusionistically modeled to look like relief. But the most striking feature is the gamut of discordant colors—strawberry pink, purple, red, flesh tones, and a bright metallic blue. In *Woman with Fan II* the anonymous face of the mannequinlike figure, flanked by classical columns and set in a space governed by a deliberately skewed perspective, once again brings to mind de Chirico's paintings (fig. 20). The rounded relief elements are the right arm, right thigh, chest, left breast (the other one is a painted circle), head, and architectural element at the upper right. Shiny oil paint in bizarre combinations of orange, ochre, gray-white, dark gray, blue, and green fills the remaining areas of the composition.

Bather, also of 1915 (cat. no. 23), is a freestanding piece constructed of modeled plaster and papier-mâché. It is one of two known surviving examples of the second variety of sculpto-painting (see also cat. no. 30), of which Archipenko seems to have made only six. These could more accurately be called "picto-sculpture," as the procedure of the sculpto-painting is reversed: instead of enhancing the two-dimensional medium with relief, the three-dimensional medium of sculpture is heightened by the addition of illusionistic effects of paint. *Bather* is described by Hildebrandt in the following passage of 1923:

Archipenko has also had the audacity of representing a bather surrounded by air and water; a yellow-brown figure, enveloped in a shade of blue, that by means of gradations both vivid and delicate, passes into violet and green.[45]

Modeling is kept to a minimum within the amorphous contours of *Bather*. The general forms of the figure are outlined and only one arm and a rounded shoulder project beyond the unified mass. Everything else is painted in—a white towel, blue water and air, shading for rounded thighs and knees, and geometric outlines to simulate relief elements similar to those used in the panel sculpto-paintings. This double punning (also present in Picasso's post-collage paintings, where painted areas are made to look like pasted papers) becomes all the more apparent when we realize that the modeled plaster bather and the panel sculpto-painting of the same subject (fig. 19) are pendants; they are the mirror image of each other in their poses as well as in the reversal of the equation sculpture/painting to painting/sculpture.

Archipenko's work with sculpto-paintings culminates in 1920 with two tall, narrow panels, one just over, the other just under six feet tall. In both he used sheet metal extensively, unpainted and highly reflective in *Woman* (cat. no. 31), and polychromed in *Two Women* (cat. no. 32). The former is composed of a few pieces of cut, bent, and curved sheet metal that create a tapering figure set against a background of clearly defined large areas painted brown, teal, and beige. In its general form and in its economy of means (uncommon for Archipenko), *Woman* recalls an oversized collage by Picasso (*Guitar*, 1919, The Museum of Modern Art, New York), with a narrow diamond shape whose points touch the top and bottom of the frame.

Archipenko reported the sale of *Woman* in a letter written from Geneva in early 1921.[46] The buyer, it is inferred, was the German-Swiss collector, George Falk, whom Archipenko may have met on an earlier trip to Switzerland in 1919. Falk became Archipenko's most important early collector; he amassed a sizable group of thirty or more works. Falk's collection, or part of it, was purchased by the German collector Erich Goeritz in the mid-1920s, and a large part of it was subsequently bequeathed to the Tel Aviv Museum.[47]

The second sculpto-painting, *Two Women*, was for a long time believed to be lost or destroyed. It has recently surfaced and has entered the collection of the Belgrade National Museum from the estate of the avant-garde publisher Ljubomir Micić (1895–1971). Micić probably acquired the work after his move to France in 1926 and took it to Yugoslavia when he returned home from Paris on the eve of World War II.[48]

In contrast to *Woman*, the Belgrade *Two Women* is opulent. It is a dense and intricate piling up of colored planes and disconnected or dislocated parts that somehow add up to the forms of two women. The style is cubist in every way. Yet, at the same time, the straight-edged geometric shapes next to swelling curves, flat areas of color adjoining undulating sheet metal that protrudes, shades of brown (from reddish to khaki), teal, yellow, pink, and rust against an olive background, are some of the startling elements of this work which, more than any other, bespeaks Archipenko's native country.

Unlike many of his compatriots, Archipenko left Russia at an early age and never returned. The effect Russia had on him seems to have been deep-seated and unconscious. It has often been noted that Archipenko's sculpto-paintings may ultimately be rooted in the tradition of Russian icon painting.[49] The icon was, no doubt, a readily available and familiar precedent for the incorporation of extraneous materials with a colorful pictorial surface. But more important, Archipenko's sculpto-

paintings, and to some degree his sculpture, may reflect qualities of his early experience of the architecture and the decorative arts of Russia.

The sculpto-painting *Two Women* is an accumulation of superimposed layers, protruding forms, flat cutouts, geometric shapes, surface pattern, and bright color. The most famous of Russian buildings, St. Basil's in Moscow (fig. 21), can be described in similar terms as *Two Women*. Built in the sixteenth century for Czar Ivan the Terrible, it is outrageously polychromatic and profanely festive. Its architectural massing is a picturesque agglomeration of overlapping towers and bulbous domes alternately decorated with straight and curved patterns. Similar also is the unusual range of intense colors, from rust-red to mustard yellow, green, and blue. In its abundance of color, St. Basil's is a stylistically unique building (once seen it is not likely to be forgotten), but the attention paid to surface articulation rather than tectonics is a common characteristic of Russian design. Another popular hallmark of Russian architecture is the onion-shaped dome. Might not Archipenko's repeated use of an arabesque contour in the female torso, present throughout his oeuvre, be regarded as a lingering souvenir of this familiar Russian motif?

In addition to his concentration on sculpto-paintings, during the war years Archipenko also made conventional sculpture like the two versions of *Vase Woman*, 1919 (cat. no. 28). The vase as analogous to the female figure is an academic tradition;[50] here it is meant literally—Archipenko left a cavity inside the figures, actually intending them to hold water.[51] The vases are narrow vertical forms that widen gently in the middle and taper sharply at the top and bottom. Anatomical detail is limited: a vertical ridge marking the separation between the legs rises diagonally to the right to indicate the groin and then drops down the side to suggest one arm; the other arm is a small finlike projection; the heads are horseshoe shapes open at the top. In *Vase Woman II*, a single flat, round shape stands for one breast; in place of the other breast is a narrow vertical groove. The tapered lower end of the figure is inserted into a slanting base that initiates the movement upward.

Vase Woman is a variation on the theme of the tapering frontal figure that began with *Flat Torso*, and occupied Archipenko in the intervening years (examples are *Statuette*, 1915 and *Egyptian Motif*, 1917). *Vase Woman* brings to mind Brancusi's *Yellow Bird*, 1919 (fig. 22), one example in his series of soaring vertical forms. Archipenko visited Brancusi's studio in 1910[52] but could then only have seen *Maiastra*, a squat bird with a big bulging midsection. The more attenuated works in the Bird series, 1915–1921, some made during the war when Archipenko was in the south of France, were not exhibited before 1920.[53] These reduced, tapering forms were the natural outcome of a gradual parallel development over a period of years for Brancusi and Archipenko.

In retrospect, the years 1913 and 1914 stand out as the creative highpoint of Archipenko's early period. His most successful and important sculptures, among them some unqualified masterpieces, like *Carrousel Pierrot*, *Médrano II*, and *Boxing*, were created in these two years. Incorporated into these works are all of the significant sculptural innovations that earned Archipenko a position among the handful of pioneers of modern sculpture. His contributions, in summary, were threefold: he initiated the opening-up of sculpture, not just by piercing a hole into it, but by presenting an alternative to the traditional notion of the monolith that merely displaces space—his sculpture surrounds and encloses

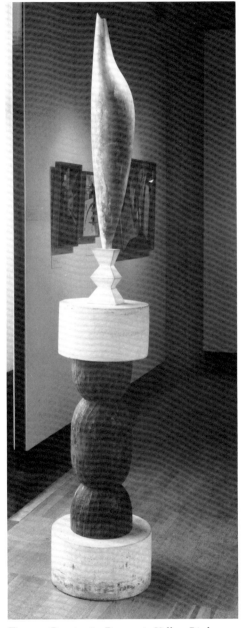

Fig. 22. Constantin Brancusi, *Yellow Bird* (1919), yellow marble, 36⅜ (92.4) h., Yale University Art Gallery, Bequest of Katherine S. Dreier to the Collection Société Anonyme.

45

Fig. 23. Alexander Archipenko, c. 1919.

space; he reintroduced color into sculpture, both overall, unified color that minimizes the role of representation and establishes the sculpture's self-sufficiency as an object, as well as color used for optical effects or as a means of clarifying structure; and he explored the use of planar materials like sheet metal and plywood, which required a new schematic, rather than descriptive, approach to sculptural mass. Finally, he was a born tinkerer who created a medium of his own, the sculpto-painting. Quite casually he introduced into sculpture a number of novelties like transparent glass, reflective metal and mirrors, a photograph, inscribed words, and movable parts. Archipenko was a man of intuitive sensibility and idiosyncratic talent, who was seemingly unencumbered by aesthetic doctrines or formal strictures. True, his commitment to innovation, and what appears to have been a certain intellectual restlessness, constantly propelled him on; he did not stay long with an idea, or as it turned out, remain in one place for any length of time. But in the fertile artistic environment of Paris, under the aegis of cubism, Archipenko was always among the first to perceive a new possibility in sculpture and initiate its development.

II.

AFTER THE WAR Archipenko returned to Paris (fig. 23). How impatient he must have been to pursue the auspicious beginning he had made in 1914 can be deduced from the almost manic activity of the years 1919 to 1923: eight one-man exhibitions, a change of residence, marriage, an abrupt shift in style, numerous publications, and emigration.

He resumed his busy exhibition schedule in May 1919 with ten sculptures in a large group show in Paris.[1] He was active in the cubists' post-war efforts to rally their forces and participated with them in the 1920 Salon des Indépendants and in the Section d'Or exhibitions in Paris, Rotterdam, The Hague, and Amsterdam. He founded with Gleizes and Léopold Survage an association named *La Section d'Or,* which comprised painters, sculptors, musicians, and writers of all nationalities; its aim was to organize exhibitions and performances in France and abroad. (Archipenko was in charge of foreign exhibitions; the other members of the board of directors were Braque, Ferat, Léger, and Marcoussis.)[2] In late 1919 Archipenko traveled to Switzerland for a large one-man exhibition in Zürich and Geneva.[3] In April 1920 he was in Venice for the opening of the *Mostra Individuale di Alexandre Archipenko* in the Venice Biennale (fig. 24).

Archipenko's whirlwind activity in these years can be traced from his correspondence with Marcel Duchamp and Katherine S. Dreier.[4] In November 1919 Duchamp had taken Dreier to Archipenko's Paris studio to see his work. The following April she wrote to him proposing an exhibition in New York at the Société Anonyme, Inc., an international organization she was founding with Duchamp and Man Ray to introduce the work of progressive artists to America. The exhibition,

Fig. 24. Archipenko exhibition, Russian pavilion, Venice Biennale, 1920.

planned for October 1920, did not open until February 1921 because
Archipenko needed time to assemble and ship the works to New York.

Archipenko welcomed the opportunity to exhibit in New York. It was
flattering to be told by Duchamp (8 April 1920) that "New York needs to
see what you have done these last years," and to hear from Dreier (18
June 1920) that his successes in Venice did not surprise her as the works
she had seen in Paris had left "a deep impression." Archipenko, of
course, was concerned about sales. In early January 1921 he proudly reported to Duchamp the sale of his large sculpto-painting *Woman* (cat.
no. 31), as well as of several other works (16 January). Because the Société Anonyme had no commercial involvement, Duchamp and Dreier
arranged to have a gallery represent Archipenko in New York.

Archipenko sent thirty-three works to New York: ten drawings, seven watercolors, ten sculptures (in plaster, cement, and terra-cotta), and six sculpto-paintings. The latter two categories were valued at $1,000 and $1,200 per work by Archipenko, but he had to reduce this amount by thirty percent when Dreier cabled him (26 January 1921) that "terracottas cannot be sold at $1,000." In the end, the lengthy negotiations about prices and percentages that followed were useless as, except for a watercolor that Dreier purchased for $100,[5] nothing was sold.

The lack of sales was no reflection of the attention the show attracted. Dreier seemed satisfied with the exhibition and reported to Archipenko on 6 February 1921:

I wish you were here to see the interest with which your exhibition is being received in New York. The writers all feel that it is the most important exhibition which was held this season and I cannot tell you how gratified Duchamp and I are with the results.

She and Duchamp had put considerable effort into the show. They published a ten-page illustrated catalogue with an English translation of a text by Iwan Goll. Duchamp designed a witty full-page ad with a photograph of *Woman* which appeared in *Arts* (fig. 25). (Despite the fine print at the bottom of the page stating that this was a "caricature of a modern magazine advertisement," the Société Anonyme received two letters requesting information about the ingenious new product of the "Archie Pen Co.")

Finally, Dreier organized a symposium on 16 February 1921 on "The Psychology of Modern Art and Archipenko," with Marsden Hartley and Man Ray as two of the speakers. The review in the *Herald* (20 February 1921), titled "A Pow-Wow at the Anonyme," reads:

Mr. Hartley was the only one of the speakers whose words bore directly upon the art of Archipenko. He said that he was sick of the word "art" and no longer cared for the "beautiful." Archipenko's conception of a woman, as exemplified in the works of art upon the walls of the Société Anonyme had all the incomparable beauty of modern plumbing, except, of course, that "beauty" wasn't the word. Although not a plumber, Mr. Hartley said he loved plumbing. Plumbing was the one incontestable contribution that modern life had given to humanity.

(Hartley's reference to plumbing must have been prompted by the tubular shapes of the limbs of the women in some of Archipenko's sculpto-paintings.)

Sculpto-painting, a new art-form, was singled out by art critics. A headline in the *New York Evening Post* (29 January 1921) announces Archipenko's "recipe": "Take a little of two arts and not too much of either." The reviewer, David Lloyd, writes, "Interrupted outcrops of high-relief in polychrome jut from his pigmented canvas," and comments that on first view the sculpto-paintings appear to be "the smattering of children's building blocks glued to a soberly hued game of jack straws."

All six sculpto-paintings shown in the Société Anonyme exhibitions were dated 1920 and had apparently been made specifically for the show. Unlike the early sculpto-paintings—fanciful compositions where relief forms merge with illusionistic pictorial effects—these later ones are simply modeled, polychromed plaster reliefs on plain flat backgrounds (for example, fig. 26). Expediency probably dictated this development: these reliefs were both faster to make and easier to transport. Archipenko was under prodigious production pressure in 1920. The thirty-three works for the New York show had to be put together between June, the time he returned to Paris from Venice, and November, when the shipment was dispatched. (Thirty-five sculptures remained on exhibit at the Venice Biennale.) At the same time, he was also assembling a large number of works for his German tour exhibition the following spring. Archipenko's production of four almost identical versions of a drawing made in 1920 exemplifies the degree to which he had overextended himself.[6]

Along with his sculpto-paintings, another feature of Archipenko's

Fig. 26. Alexander Archipenko, *Standing Woman* (1919), oil and painted plaster relief on wood panel, 18⅜ x 11½ (46.4 x 29.2), The Phillips Collection, Washington.

Fig. 27. Archipenko traveling exhibition, Germany, 1921.

work noted by the American press was the hole. Henry McBride reports in the *New York Herald* (6 February 1921), "Instead of doing the thing Archipenko does the absence of it. Don't you believe it? Go see the show." News of this innovation reached as far as St. Paul, Minnesota, whose *Pioneer Press* reports (12 February 1921):

Another Cubist has them running rings inside circles in New York. His name is no other than Mr. Archipenko, the latest European novelty who is making his first American appearance at the Society Anoname [sic], New York. Mr. Archipenko expresses himself by the absence of things. Do you get that? Instead of painting a woman's breast or a man's head he paints a hole. He expresses their non-being as well as their being. Rather cosmic, is he not?

With the exception of the six sculpto-paintings that remained in the United States for a group show at the Worcester Art Museum, the sculptures in the Société Anonyme exhibition were taken back to Paris by Duchamp in June 1921. Except for the work Dreier bought and another that Archipenko gave her as a gift,[7] the drawings and watercolors were also presumably returned at this time.

How Archipenko reacted to the tongue-in-cheek tone of many of the articles and clippings that Dreier sent him is not known. In any event, by this time his attention was focused on Germany. Although he kept his Paris studio at 77, rue (today avenue) Denfert Rochereau, from early 1921 on he lived in Berlin. That year he accompanied his Der Sturm exhibition on its tour of five German cities (fig. 27) and held a retrospective in Potsdam. In 1922, in a two-man show with Feininger in Frankfurt, Archipenko exhibited over seventy works. That same year he also participated in the Galerie Van Diemen exhibition of Russian art in Berlin. In 1923, before departing for the United States, Archipenko held a one-man show in Prague, where he stayed on for several weeks to work on a bust of President Masaryk of Czechoslovakia.

A measure of Archipenko's great popularity in Europe at this time is the amount of literary attention he received—no less than six Archipenko monographs were published between 1921 and 1924. The first of these, *Archipenko Album*, includes a poem by Blaise Cendrars dedicated to Archipenko in Nice in 1918, essays by Theodor Daübler and Iwan Goll, and over thirty illustrations. Excerpts from Goll's essay were reprinted in two Hungarian avant-garde periodicals, *Horizont* and *Ma*.[8] The latter was enthusiastically praised by László Moholy-Nagy, the Hungarian artist, in a 1921 letter:

What *Ma* is doing is the best which can be published in Hungarian today. One should spit on it? Did you see the Archipenko issue, with 15 illustrations? Can you suggest something better than that?[9]

(Another piece by Goll, for the French journal *Action* in 1920, appeared in English in the catalogue of Archipenko's Société Anonyme exhibition in New York.)

Maurice Raynal is the author of an illustrated text on Archipenko published in Rome in 1923. In his essay Raynal bemoans the state of contemporary sculpture and dwells on the difficulties of achieving true originality in a medium that is so physically present because of its three-dimensionality. He believes that the cubist aesthetic cannot successfully be applied to sculpture and reverses his earlier positive opinion on sculpto-painting (in the preface to the catalogue of Archipenko's 1919–1920 Swiss traveling exhibition). He ends on a critical note:

Archipenko's generally baroque art is strewn with curious inventions, brilliant improvisations, and an often refined tenderness, but it is slightly disappointing because the ingenious means he employs make his works seem more like those of an extremely skilled craftsman than those of an artist who is sure of his intentions and of his aesthetic vision. I have written that Archipenko has often invented new lights, this I believe to be true, but it's a pity he turns them on only in broad daylight.[10]

Another monograph, by Hans Hildebrandt, was published in 1923 and translated into English, French, Ukrainian, and Spanish. The comprehensive text offers biographical data, suggestions for sources of early influence, and an analysis of artistic development. Hildebrant discusses Archipenko's use of the torso, the mechanical element that enters some of his experiments, and his introduction of materials—such as papier-mâché, wood, and metals—in his sculpto-paintings. He stresses Archipenko's revolutionary use of space and hollows.

Erich Wiese's small illustrated book, volume 40 of the series *Junge Kunst*, was published in Leipzig in 1923. The text includes quotes from the artist about his student years in Kiev, Moscow, and Paris, as well as a discussion of some aspects of his art.

Archipenko—Plastique Nouvelle is the title of an album-monograph that appeared in Belgrade in 1923. The publisher of this graphically ambitious volume with fifteen tipped-in illustrations was Ljubomir Micić, founder of the avant-garde periodical *Zenit*, where Archipenko's name had been appearing since shortly after its inception in February 1921. Due to his exposure in *Zenit* (and Archipenko's friendship with Micić's brother, the poet and painter Branko Ve Poljanski), in Yugoslavia Archipenko was considered the most important among the vanguard artists of the 1920s. In his preface, Micić hails Archipenko as an exponent of the new sculpture of "Zenitism," inspired by the age of technology, electricity, and the airplane, as well as by "Balkan savageries and the rolling of the presses."[11]

Finally, in 1924, the *Sturm Bilderbücher II* (originally published in 1917) was enlarged to include illustrations of recent works and a text by Roland Schacht that traces the different stages of Archipenko's development.

Archipenko's long-standing association with Der Sturm, his presence in Berlin, and his active participation in the artistic life of the German capital (he had opened a highly successful art school in 1921) led to his extraordinary success in Germany in the early 1920s. Iwan Goll, for instance, equated Archipenko's contribution to modern sculpture with Picasso's to modern painting and singled out these two artists as the true leaders of the century.[12] Others felt that Archipenko shared with two other Russians, Chagall and Kandinsky, the key positions in the history of revolutionary art.[13] And another author wrote:

In discussing problems of modern sculpture, we must first of all mention Archipenko. Not only is he superior to his more or less gifted contemporaries in quality and spiritual form, he is also the most varied and creative sculptor. The strength of his inspiration cannot be better proven than by the large number of his imitators.[14]

According to the discerning and thoughtful artist-observer Oskar Schlemmer, Archipenko was someone to watch. Schlemmer mentioned Archipenko three times in his published diaries. In 1915 he regarded Archipenko, Lehmbruck, and the cubist painters as the "ideal-

ists of form." An entry in 1919 reads:

The drawbacks of our times: mediocrity, conformism; expressionism, paucity of original talent. Kandinsky, Marc, Chagall, Klee, Archipenko, Picasso are the few really original talents.

And finally, in 1925 he writes: "I arrived at abstraction—Picasso, Archipenko and others. The essential element: simple forms."[15]

Archipenko's marriage in 1921 to Angelica Schmitz (1893–1957) may also have contributed to his success in Germany. Famed for her beauty (Archipenko made a number of portraits that show her imposing profile, fig. 28), Schmitz was an expressionist sculptor who exhibited under the name Gela Forster. She was a founding member, and the only woman, of the Sezession Gruppe 1919 of Dresden that also included Otto Dix, Conrad Felixmüller, and Ludwig Meidner.[16] Her grand-father, Bonaventura Genelli (1789–1868), was a Berlin-born neoclassi-cal painter of narrative picture sets, and her father, Bruno Schmitz

(1858–1916), was a prominent Berlin architect, who became famous as the creator of several bombastic architectural monuments to Kaiser Wilhelm.[17] With this background she could offer Archipenko a solid position in the social and artistic establishment of Berlin.

Until her death in 1957 Archipenko continued to be held in thrall by his tall blond aristocratic German wife.[18] Although the heavyset virile Archipenko was an inveterate womanizer and had numerous mistresses, by all accounts Angelica was the woman he was really tied to. An over-powering Brunhilde type, she was ambitious and set great store in being known as Madame Archipenko. She was cold, composed, and sophisti-cated. He was sentimental, with peasantlike behavior, thick hands, and a terrible temper. She had the airs of a great lady; he was frugal and could dispense with all luxuries. They fought violently and lived apart for long periods of time. But to the end Archipenko felt responsible for her. During the long illness that preceded her death, he financed her costly treatment for high blood pressure, and by his own admission, fell in love with her all over again when she was in a wheelchair.[19]

Coinciding with his marriage and move to Berlin came a sudden sty-listic change in his work. Archipenko abandoned his bold, innovative experiments of the previous decade and assumed a mannered natural-istic style (fig. 29). Although not without precedent in his own work (see for example, *Kneeling Woman*, cat. no. 2), the languorously posed sleek female figures of the next few years correspond to local taste. Illustra-tions in a German periodical like *Die Kunst* in the years 1920 to 1923 show a great number of vaguely classicizing, naturalistic nudes in grace-ful poses.[20] Archipenko's style, however, does not seem to have met with much critical favor. In 1924 Hildebrandt, author of the monograph of the previous year, notes that it was both easier to understand and easier to sell works that maintain a close link with nature, and he faults Archi-penko for "bending his great talent under the yoke of public taste which always favors sweet prettiness and a style of virtuoso naturalism."[21]

Another author who criticized Archipenko's works was Carl Ein-stein. In *Die Kunst des XX Jahrhunderts* (Berlin, 1926), he devotes a full four pages to Archipenko, but the tone of his evaluation is negative:

With Archipenko, despite all originality, there is always a reference to a con-temporary model. At first he varies archaic material with surprising skill, and later he follows close by on the trail of the developments and peripatetics of Pi-casso. He is always on hand at every innovation, arriving without noticeable delay; no matter whether it is archaism or discovery, he shows up precisely sec-ond. Even in novelty a charming virtuosity remains. He breaks up form but maintains the alluring outlines of academic salon art; he surrounds a bold ven-ture with a sweet silhouette.[22]

Fig. 29. Alexander Archipenko, *Figure* (1921), bronze, 25¾ (65.5) h., Private Collection, Lon-don.

Fig. 30. Alexander and Angelica Archipenko on board the S.S. *Mongolia* en route to New York, October 1923.

Barely two years after his arrival in Berlin, in January 1923, Archipenko decided to leave for America. Perhaps he felt that his reputation was waning, but the principal reason, it seems, was to escape the economic and social crisis in Europe. He wrote a long letter to Katherine Dreier announcing his decision and soliciting her support (17 January 1923):

I have decided to leave insane Europe. Life here is becoming more and more unbearable for a man who devotes himself to creation. I can no longer work in this atmosphere. The pleasure of work remains, but the goal seems to be farther and farther away. One does not know in the morning what will happen in the evening. I have decided to go to America with my wife. We creative people feel that our effort is useless in a place that is destined for catastrophe. It is useless to create, to make an effort, if everything will be stamped out and demolished anyway. Vulgar materialism is a bad environment for us. Europe is inevitably becoming materialistic if the only goal of each person is to find a piece of bread and save his life. I think America is also a very materialistic country, but at least one's life is guaranteed and that's a lot in our stupid times. America has become my "*idée fixe*" and I think only of my departure. I am sure that the time is approaching when artistic strength will be concentrated in America.

Archipenko asks Dreier to organize an exhibition of salable bronzes and marbles in April and suggests that the works be auctioned off at the end to raise money for his trip. He also asks her to help him find a space where he can start a school modeled after his popular one in Berlin and wonders if the necessary capital might not be raised through her connections, with his works serving as collateral. Realizing the difficulty of obtaining an entry visa as a Russian, he requests her to send him a letter of invitation, stating that his presence in the United States is essential for the success of the exhibition. He follows up this bold letter with a second more urgent one five days later (23 January 1923), in which he asks that Dreier have a telegram sent to the American consulate in Berlin requesting visas for his wife and himself. He declares that he is liquidating his affairs, giving up his Paris studio, and closing his school in Berlin: "I am selling everything and I am leaving, it is absolutely decided."

Understandably, Dreier did not answer Archipenko's letters immediately. As she explains to him a few months later (2 April 1923), she cannot take the responsibility of having him come to the United States on her advice alone. She reports that although the interest in modern art is growing steadily, very little sells, and that it is hard to make a living as an artist in America if one is not "banal." She tells him she cannot plan on an exhibition before the fall and offers to store his work for him. In the meantime, however, Archipenko somehow made all the arrangements for his departure: he secured visas and the support of the American ambassador; plans for the school were underway; and he and his wife had been offered a house near New York City where they could spend the summer.

On 6 October the Archipenkos sailed for New York on the S.S. *Mongolia*. A photograph taken on board shows a well-dressed, prosperous-looking couple (fig. 30). The thirty-six-year-old Archipenko—debonair in tweed overcoat and cap, starched collar, and spats—stands next to his wife, who sports a smart hat and fox boa. Gone is the despair of his Berlin letters—Archipenko looks self-assured and confident of the future.

III.

Alexander Archipenko arrived yesterday on the Mongolia. . . . He is considered by many persons the greatest living sculptor, and recently closed a school in Berlin to which students came from all over the world. He will give exhibitions in the principal cities of the United States this winter, and is desirous of founding in New York "the only modern art school in the world," because, he says, he feels America, which is so fresh and vital and is the only country not jaded and rent by the war, is the place to look for the great art of the future. . . . The sculptor is above medium height, robust, gentle, suave, with a strong Slavic face and the eager eyes of the artist. When asked how long he was going to stay he answered, "Perhaps forever!" (*The World*, New York, 17 November 1923)

TWO WEEKS AFTER his arrival in America, Archipenko was off to Washington to work on portrait busts of Secretary of State Charles Evans Hughes and Senator Medill McCormick of Illinois (fig. 31). Katherine Dreier had not wasted any time arranging these sittings, and she even accompanied Archipenko and his wife to Washington. She was also busy planning his Société Anonyme-sponsored exhibition at the Kingore Gallery in New York. (Mr. Kingore, according to Dreier, had an active clientele and he also had great influence in California.) That things did not seem to be moving fast enough for Archipenko, however, can be deduced from Dreier's 29 November letter to him:

I have done so much for you that I feel you should have, or maybe you have, but do not always show, the full confidence which I have the right to expect. If it were not for my admiration for your work I would not trouble. I have given almost the entire month to arranging an exhibition for you, and if to make it the most important exhibition of this winter takes a little time, you must have just a little more patience.

Dreier does seem to have been tireless in her efforts to promote the Archipenko exhibition and drew on her wide ranging contacts in the museum and society worlds to make the "private view" of the opening a big event. Engraved invitations were sent out and she managed to assemble a reception committee consisting of four museum directors (from Detroit, Chicago, Worcester, and Buffalo), society ladies, the critic Henry McBride, and the famed theater personality Countess Matchabelli, whose planned recitation of a manifesto on modern art was cancelled because, according to McBride's report in the *New York Herald* (27 January 1925), Dreier feared it might have been too radical.

McBride marvels at "the mysterious attraction that brought these people together," wonders "what particular perfume or vibration" radiates from Archipenko's work "so as to anticipate the normal workings of publicity," and comments favorably on those works in the exhibition that bear "the tang of the modern accent." He singles out the statuettes that registered "the absence of a thing rather than the presence of a thing," and was also pleased by the combination of color and relief in Archipenko's sculpto-paintings. The catalogue, which McBride called "a stylistic thing in itself" (on the cover two gilded bands carried Archipenko's name in Roman and Cyrillic letters), was illustrated and had an introduction by Dr. Christian Brinton. A free-lance critic who specialized in Russian art, Brinton had organized the large exhibition of Russian painting and sculpture at the Brooklyn Museum the previous year.[1] In his essay he describes Archipenko as a "convinced and convincing protestant"—a quality which he was said to share with Marinetti and Picasso—and his art, as "a perfect embodiment of plastic absolutism."

The reviews of the exhibition were negative for the most part. In *The Art News* (26 January 1924) the sculpto-paintings were termed "willful eccentricities" and the marbles and bronzes said to have "purposed distortions." Another writer declared that the modern movement had found in the work of Archipenko "an academic formula," and criticized it for its "capable but bleak austerity unrelieved anywhere by a touch of instinctive warmth" (*New York World*, 27 January 1924). The critic of the *New York Herald Tribune* (27 January 1924) said Archipenko was a good craftsman, but that as an artist he gave "a dubious reward," and asserted that there was "no real eloquence in his interminable legs, his twisted torsos, and his 'abstract' heads." "They impress the beholder," he continued, "as only poor in proportion, freakish in meaning and, as regards their polished technique, expressive of nothing so much as wasted skill." Ralph Fling, writing for *The Christian Science Monitor* (28 January 1924), felt that only "under the smoke-screen of eccentric elongations," could the viewer discover "the pulsating rhythms and harmonious modulations of a true lover of beauty." Even the traditionally modeled busts of the Washington politicians met with disapproval: some thought they were "compelling" (*New York Evening Post*, 26 January 1924), while others said they looked like the work of a promising art student (*New York Tribune*, 27 January 1924).

The Société Anonyme exhibition was made up of six sculpto-paintings, thirty sculptures (almost exclusively marbles and bronzes—Archipenko had learned from his first exhibition in New York that plasters and terracottas didn't sell well), five paintings, two etchings, and twenty drawings. Two-thirds of the sculptures were recent works in the naturalistic style Archipenko had begun to practice in Berlin. Five examples were illustrated in the January issue of *Arts* that also carried a short essay by Archipenko titled "Nature, the Point of Departure." Yet, despite all the publicity, the carefully planned selection of works, and the gallery owner's moneyed California connections, there were no

Fig. 31. Alexander Archipenko, *Senator Medill McCormick* (1923), bronze, Private Collection, Chicago.

sales. Actually, one sale was made; the Société Anonyme itself bought a piece listed in the catalogue as *Woman. Various Metals, 1923. Model of a Decorative Panel for a Metal Room.* This purchase was settled against a bank loan to Archipenko which Dreier had endorsed personally.

Woman (cat. no. 33) is the third in the series of large sculpto-paintings employing metal (see cat. nos. 31 and 32): the Tel Aviv sculpto-painting is severe and hieratic; the one from Belgrade is a rich chromatic jumble; and Dreier's "metal lady" is pretty and pat. It is a skillful but facile recapitulation of features from various works of the preceding decade—serpentine silhouette, slashed shoulder zig-zag, wavy lines, pointillist texture, cone-shaped lower torso, and tapering base. The cubist style has been digested and sweetened. In fact, the shiny brass and copper lady is almost a pure art deco artifact. Archipenko may have felt that he had exhausted the possibilities of the medium; more than thirty years would pass before he made another sculpto-painting.

Archipenko's reactions to the exhibition can be inferred from Dreier's letter to him (10 February 1924):

I am extremely sorry that your disappointment in not selling should have been so keen. . . . I think it was too bad though that your disappointment should make you appear rude, for the Société tried in every way to aid you and we spent so much more money on your exhibition than we generally do that we had the right to expect some appreciation for all we have done. Sincerely hoping that this unfriendliness which you now have shown to us will blow over and that with the aid of Dr. Brinton you will still make some sales at your studio which will cause your sun to shine once more.

There is no record of an answer, but Dreier included Archipenko in the large international exhibition she organized at the Brooklyn Museum in 1926,[2] and they remained on cordial terms thereafter.

The hardships of Archipenko's first few years in the United States are reflected in the correspondence he and his wife had with Galka Scheyer.[3] In 1924 in Weimar, Scheyer had created The Blue Four, an exhibition group consisting of Feininger, Jawlensky, Kandinsky, and Klee.[4] With her move to the United States that same year, Scheyer became their representative in this country. After spending some months in New York, she settled permanently in California. The principal topics of the three-way correspondence between the Archipenkos and Scheyer (his letters are in blissfully ungrammatical French, while the two women corresponded in German) are money and work. The former concerned a loan of $140 from Scheyer to the Archipenkos, which was paid back with difficulty over a period of three years in thirty- to forty-dollar installments requested from time to time by Scheyer to pay the dentist or to buy a new coat. Archipenko had opened a school in New York in 1924 and must have had some income from teaching,[5] but his works were evidently not selling. In August 1925 he apologizes to Scheyer for being unable to send her the forty dollars she asked for and bitterly adds that he is as always "very disgusted" with this country, and that it has been "the greatest stupidity" of his life to have remained in America (31 August 1925).

In addition to having helped him financially, Scheyer also tried to promote Archipenko's work in California. In January 1926 Archipenko turned down her offer to show his graphics and drawings in an exhibition in California, writing that, instead, he has made an important engagement with someone who will be handling his work for the next five years (25 January 1926). The nature and duration of this arrangement are unknown, but its effects must have been beneficial because, in the summer of the same year, Archipenko's spirits were higher; writing from Woodstock, New York, he now looked upon Europe as "a charming souvenir." Except for planned occasional short visits to Paris, he now decided to remain in the United States (14 July 1926).

In April 1927 Archipenko informs Scheyer that his traveling show has been a success in Denver, is presently in Los Angeles, and is scheduled to go to Oakland and San Diego. He wonders about these cities' "capacity for the comprehension of art" and is once again not reconciled to living in America. His letter ends as follows, "With California I think I will close the circle of my exhibitions in America and I think I will move to a country that is more friendly to modern art" (21 April 1927). The following year, however, Archipenko applied for American citizenship.

In her letter to Scheyer of 18 October 1928 Angelica gives an enthusiastic account of the opening of an exhibition at the Anderson Galleries in New York, where Archipenko unveiled his *Archipentura* (fig. 34a-b). Pronouncing it the most beautiful exhibition she has ever seen, she writes, "And the machine, all covered in silver, works wonderfully; everyone is delighted." As there had already been some interesting offers, she expresses the hope that some business will result from *Archipentura*. As for the sculpture and paintings, Angelica writes, it is impossible to tell if they will sell.

The Anderson Galleries exhibition in October 1928 was an ambitious undertaking by one of the galleries that was chiefly responsible for bringing avant-garde art to New York in the 1920s.[6] The twenty-page illustrated catalogue produced for the exhibition includes a description of *Archipentura*, three pages of quotations from the press, a bibliography, and a list of exhibitions. The catalogue lists fifty sculptures (predominantly marbles and bronzes), eleven ceramics, three sculpto-paintings, thirty-five paintings, and seventeen drawings. Of the sculptures the majority was from the 1920s, with those from the period 1909–1920 numbering about one dozen.

Among the recent works were three portrait busts (of Thorton Wilder and of conductors Willem Mengelberg and Wilhelm Furtwängler)—dynamic sketches in bronze with expressive, almost baroque outlines (fig. 32). The remainder of the sculpture, most dating from 1925 and 1926, consisted of single and paired figures (for example, fig. 33) with long legs, high short waists, tapering ankles, and often peculiar bulging insteps above soles that stick flat to the base. The surfaces are sometimes smooth and shiny—several silvered and gilded bronzes are listed in the catalogue—and sometimes grainy. In some figures the highly polished surfaces of the body are offset by the rough texture of a piece of drapery. The long, flat heads are frequently bent toward a raised shoulder creating a diagonal that is repeated by the line of the hips. Knees are often tightly pressed together. If hands are visible, the fingers are long and snakelike. In some cases, as in *Glorification of Beauty* (1925), face, breasts, hips, and thighs are expressed by concavities, a formal device that by this time has become a predictable mannerism. The titles—*The Graceful Movement, Feminine Solitude, Spring Torso, Melancholy, Onward*, and *Diana*, for example—are fully in keeping with the languid sentimentality of these figures.

Fig. 32. Alexander Archipenko, *Portrait of Wilhelm Furtwängler* (1927), plaster, c. 36 (91) h., location unknown.

Fig. 33. Alexander Archipenko, *Diana* (1925), bronze, 23½ (59.7) h., Courtesy Zabriskie Gallery, New York.

For conservative art critics of the late 1920s these works were Archipenko's greatest achievement. Stanley Casson, author of *XXth Century Sculptors* (1930), regards Archipenko's sculpto-painting as a "foible" that does not succeed, but believes that his figural sculpture embodies the modern postwar canon of proportions. In Casson's opinion Archipenko is one of the founders of "the most universal style of figure representation in ultra-modern art that has been seen in Europe for nearly two hundred years." For having provided the canons by which the particular "fashion of proportions" of the day was being established, Archipenko is seen as a leader of the modern style. Casson concludes that Archipenko is to modern sculpture what Picasso is to modern painting.[7]

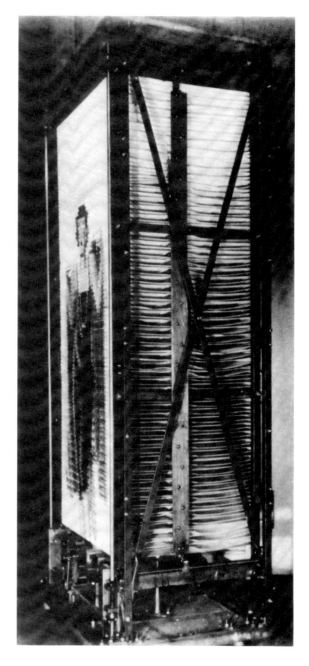

Fig. 34 a-b. Alexander Archipenko, *Archipentura*, "Apparatus for Displaying Changeable Pictures," 1927 (destroyed).

The main attraction of the Anderson Galleries exhibition was "the machine"—*Archipentura* (figs. 34 and 35). The invention had been patented the previous year, 1927,[8] and is the subject of the long essay Archipenko wrote for the catalogue. The text is subtitled "A New Development in Painting," and the invention is dedicated to "T. Edison and A. Einstein." In his introductory paragraph Archipenko states that his article is a "simple description" that is "not intended as a manifesto or a theory," but the long and grandiloquent text that follows belies this disclaimer.

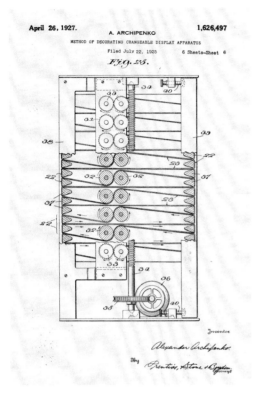

April 26, 1927.

A. ARCHIPENKO

1,626,497

METHOD OF DECORATING CHANGEABLE DISPLAY APPARATUS

Filed July 22, 1925   6 Sheets-Sheet 6

Fig. 35.

Fig. 35. Alexander Archipenko, Diagram, "Method of Decorating Changeable Display Apparatus," Patent No. 1,626,497, 26 April 1927.

Under the heading "What is Archipentura," there is a numbered list of pronouncements, such as:

Archipentura is neither a theory nor a dogma. It is an emotional creation . . .
Archipentura is differentiated from ordinary painting in that it is dynamic, and not static.
Archipentura is the concrete union of painting with time and space.
Archipentura is the most perfect form of modern art, for it has solved the problem of dynamism . . .
Archipentura is the art of painting on canvas the true action . . . of a moment given by movements.
[Archipentura] is a new means of painting done direct by the artist, in perfect subordination to his will or his creative emotions.

In the section titled "History of this Invention," Archipenko outlines the genesis of the idea. He traces it back to Paris in 1912 when he created "the animated painting 'Médrano.'" There followed experiments in Berlin in 1922 "under the influence of the Einstein theory of relativity," but it was not until 1924, in New York, "in the atmosphere of one of the most up-to-date cities of the world," that the discovery of "a new pictorial method for the execution of pictures, and a special apparatus for their demonstration" was made. Five additional sections ("Life and Painting," "Interpretation," "Movement," "Time," and "Space") expound at length on the virtues of the new invention, concluding as follows:

It is not my intention to discover the fourth dimension or to philosophize or to analyze art and artistic creation. I am simply pointing out the ideas connected with my invention, which, according to the opinion of persons well able to judge of its value, is the form of art best corresponding to our epoch. On my invention the theory of Einstein has had the greatest influence, not from the scientific side, but by the ideas given out by Einstein, which are indisputably in accord with creation in general. . . . Archipentura has no direct relations with the Einstein theory, but it is capable of expressing things of a higher order, things which, from certain aspects, undoubtedly are attached to the theories of Einstein.

Archipenko's repeated references to Einstein reflect the spirit of the times. In 1919 the special theory of relativity (1905) was validated by a photograph that showed that light rays were indeed bent by the gravitational mass of the sun, and Einstein instantly became an international celebrity.[9] From then on through the 1920s there were numerous articles in Europe and the United States explaining the theory to the layman.[10] The linking of Archipenko's work to Einstein's theory is part of the general popularization of this milestone in modern science. In the introduction to the catalogue of Archipenko's traveling exhibition of 1927, C.J. Bulliet writes that the sculptor's admirers "would place him among the mythical dozen who grasp the Einstein theory," and that he is "credited by them with applying the Einstein theory to statuary." He quotes Archipenko as follows: "I know that my knowledge of science does not suffice to understand the Einstein theory in all its aspects, but its spiritual substance is clear to me"; and further, "I have a suspicion that the theory of relativity was always hidden in art, but Einstein with his genius has made it concrete with words and units"; and finally, "My invention, 'Peinture Changeante,' I owe to the theory of relativity."[11]

Unfortunately, *Archipentura* itself has not survived. Archipenko left it in the basement of his building when he went to California in 1935; when he returned the janitor of the building had been replaced and the machine was gone.[12] Surviving photographs, patent documents, and Archipenko's description give an idea of how the machine worked:[13]

The machine has a box-like shape. Two opposite sides of it are three feet by seven feet. Each of these sides consists of 110 narrow metallic strips, three feet long and one half inch thick. The strips are installed one on top of another, similar to a Venetian blind. These two sides become the panels for the display of paintings. They are about two feet from each other, and 110 pieces of strong canvas, running horizontally encircle two oppositely fixed strips. Both ends of the canvases are fastened in the central frame located between two display panels. By mechanically moving the central frame, all 110 canvases simultaneously slide over all the metallic strips, making both panels gradually change their entire surface on which an object is painted. A new portion of specially painted canvas constantly appears. This produces the effect of true motion. A patented method of painting is used to obtain motion. An electrical mechanism in the bottom of the apparatus moves the central frame back and forth, and thousands of consecutive painted fragments appear on the surface to form a total picture. It is not the subject matter, but the changes which become the essence and lie at the origin of this invention.

From the language used—"apparatus for displaying changeable pictures" and "method for decorating changeable display apparatus" (particularly the words "displaying" and "decorating")—it is clear that despite the lofty tone of the catalogue essay, Archipenko hoped for a commercial application for his invention. Although it would have been costly and time-consuming to produce *Archipentura* in quantity, advertising and window display would have been two possible commercial uses. Despite the "interesting offers" Angelica Archipenko mentioned in her letter to Galka Scheyer, nothing came of *Archipentura*. The failure of the project into which he had invested years of work and a lot of money must have been a severe disappointment for Archipenko.

The machine did make a final appearance three years later in 1931 at an event sponsored by the Société Anonyme. *Art of the Future* was the title of an evening program organized by Katherine Dreier on 23 March 1931 at the New School for Social Research.[14] The printed program lists an address by Dreier, two film projections, and demonstrations of *Archipentura* by "artist-inventor" Alexander Archipenko and the Clavilux, played by another "artist-inventor," Thomas Wilfred. At the bottom of the program, in bold capitals, is the following statement:

Electricity, that great unknown force has become the servant to art. Duchamp's Abstract Film, Archipenko's unique chaining of the forces of electricity to serve him, all lead to that outstanding achievement of Thomas Wilfred who paints with light and whose great new invention will permit all artists to do likewise.

In general, the reviewer for *The New York Times* was not overly impressed (29 March 1931). On the subject of Archipentura he writes:

As for Mr. Archipenko, the machine whose motor he still switches on with solemn affection was exhibited several seasons back at the Anderson galleries, when to most of us, perhaps it seemed best adapted to advertising (indeed you may witness its cousins, devoted to such uses any night in the streets of New York). As for the design evolved by that ingenious set of rollers, these are about as unimaginative as the Wendel will. And Archipenko's theory that art can be dynamic only when it actually moves is certainly debatable, as a matter of fact is disproved by his own painting and sculpture, which is often immensely charged with movement.

Following his experiment with *Archipentura*, in 1929 Archipenko actually made a brief foray into a field of applied art. On the occasion of his exhibition of gilded and silvered bronzes in the newly built gallery on the fifth floor of Saks & Co., he designed six display windows for the Fifth Avenue side of the department store. As reported then in *The Art News*,[15] Archipenko believed that, previously, window display had taken the form of either pure ornamentation or the imitation of interiors; he described his new concept in more abstract terms as "a decorative structure employing rhythmic architectural motifs." The main feature of the displays, and the most interesting (as seen in the black and white photographs that are the only surviving record), was the background (fig. 36a-b), composed of thin metal sheets burnished, probably by machine, to a regular, yet blurry pattern of light and dark patches. Panels of varying sizes and shapes were arranged to create different faceted environments for each window. Some are bilateral compositions with a central focal point. In one of these, the burnished sheet metal was bent into cones—the same technique Archipenko had used in his constructions and sculpto-paintings—to form a stylized curtain effect on each side. Another window had a dramatic asymmetrical arrangement of sloping panels. While the compositions themselves do not transcend their art deco origins, Archipenko's idea of constructing bold large-scale environments from planes of sheet metal prefigures later developments in modern sculpture; one of his backgrounds (fig. 36a) seems to fore-

Fig. 36a.

shadow David Smith's late sculpture, *Becca*, 1965, not only in the burnished metal but also in the symmetrical V-shaped configuration of the parts.

The photographs of the Saks window installations forcefully bring home the general problem of scale in sculpture. Each window contained a mannequin displaying an evening gown, several stands for accessories and shoes, and in some instances, a figure by Archipenko on a pedestal. These rare views of sculpture in a contemporary setting are revealing: when seen in splendid isolation in the museum or reproduced in books, the issue of relative size never comes to our attention, but in the surroundings of the store windows the sculptures, averaging twenty inches in height, are barely distinguishable from the paraphernalia around them. In any domestic setting, small-scale sculpture too easily becomes decorative ornament. Also, accustomed as we are today to architecturally scaled works, we are more likely to see the sheet-metal backgrounds in the Saks windows as sculpture. Without intending to, perhaps Archipenko had made proto-environmental sculpture.

While he exhibited in locations as varied as Kentucky, Missouri, Iowa, and Nebraska,[16] during the thirties Archipenko lived in Hollywood, and

Fig. 36 a-b. Alexander Archipenko, Display window designs, Saks & Co., September 1929.

later, Chicago. In a 1929 letter to Galka Scheyer he stated that he was "doing pioneer work and educating the ignorant" with his forthcoming exhibitions in Chicago and California (4 February 1929). Scheyer had not been successful in her attempts to sell his ceramics, and Archipenko had become impatient with the arrangements she was trying to make with California art centers. In March 1929 he handed over his affairs to the Braxton Gallery in Hollywood where he had shows that year and in 1931. In 1932 and 1933 Archipenko taught and lectured on the west coast and in the following years showed his works in Santa Barbara, San Francisco, Oakland, and Los Angeles, as well as other cities along the coast. In 1935 he took up residence in California and opened an art school, his fourth, at 6907 Franklin Avenue in Hollywood. Angelica had preceded Archipenko to California and in 1932 was living in Santa Barbara in dire financial circumstances. Archipenko sent her money occasionally, but she was obliged to take in two boarders; in one letter to him (September 1932), she describes the humiliation of selling cosmetics door to door.

In California Archipenko worked mainly in terra-cotta and with color, often employing themes and motifs from his earlier sculptures. *Standing Vertical*, 1935 (cat. no. 34), was made in wood, terra-cotta,

Fig. 36b.

69

and hydrostone versions. It is an almost symmetrical tapering vertical form whose not-so-distant relative is *Vase Woman II*; however, as the widest point of the figure is at the shoulders and not at the hips, as in the earlier piece, *Standing Vertical* appears shrouded rather than nude. At the center of the uninterrupted smooth form is an undulating flamelike core that separates itself from the surrounding mass, creating four open spaces. The core is painted beige and where it is attached, it is outlined in red; at the very top the core becomes a shallow concavity that signifies the head. Alternating areas painted black and orange situate head and upper and lower torsos. The image of a flickering inner form imprisoned within a rigid and immobile outer shell carries strong mystical overtones, which are amplified by a feature not common for this artist—the front and back of this sculpture are the same.

Head, 1936 (cat. no. 35), is a terra-cotta painted black, white, red, blue, and yellow. Primary colors, which appear in several works of the 1930s, and the rugged simplicity of the rough and grainy surface, may reflect Archipenko's exposure to American Indian art of the Northwest. The massive, earthbound quality of the piece also recalls the early archaizing Paris works (for example, *Mother and Child*, 1910–1911 [cat. no. 3]), and is here felicitously combined with the cubist feature of a hollow representing its reverse, the volume of the face. Clearly delineated sections of contrasting color create a pattern of angular facets throughout the largely undifferentiated mass of the sculpture.

At this time, the female torso of the Paris years (compare *Flat Torso*) is reprised in terra-cotta for the west coast. Five feet tall, languorous, and softer than its Parisian counterpart, it is aptly titled *Hollywood Torso*, 1936 (fig. 37). Lying on its side, in metalized terra-cotta, it becomes *Floating Torso*, 1936. In *Seated Figure*, 1936, the speckled, polished terra-cotta torso is set against a grainy backdrop (armchair?) incised with a pattern. Other pieces showing the female figure seem to take inspiration from the motion pictures: *Josephine Bonaparte*, 1935, tall and slender, glides regally in a floor-length pink and blue gown, while *Arabian*, 1936, in red, white, and blue terra-cotta, is a curvaceous swaying figure with the black eyes of a vamp peering out from behind a red veil.

In the fall of 1937 Archipenko moved to Chicago. (He had found it difficult to work in California, he later told a student, because the landscape was too beautiful.)[17] In Chicago he opened his fifth art school and was a faculty member of the New Bauhaus that opened in October under the direction of László Moholy-Nagy. Archipenko was put in charge of the modeling workshop, where the principal materials used were glass, clay, stone, and plastics. Moholy-Nagy intended the modeling workshop to collaborate closely with the object design workshop (wood

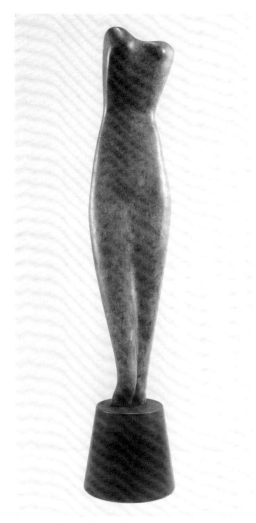

Fig. 37. Alexander Archipenko, *Hollywood Torso* (1936), bronze, 28 (71) h., Courtesy Zabriskie Gallery, New York.

and metal) in the creation of lighting and household objects. In other modeling work, plastics were to play an important role. Moholy-Nagy regarded sculpture as crucial in the education of every designer and architect, as it helped to develop an ability to work with the concepts of space and dimension and to refine tactile sensitivity.[18]

Moholy-Nagy had met Archipenko in Berlin in 1922,[19] admired his work, and published it in *Ma*, of which he was an editor. The German Bauhaus, whose faculty Moholy-Nagy joined in 1923, included Archipenko's work in one of a series of print portfolios published between 1921 and 1924. But Moholy-Nagy's specific reasons for choosing Archipenko to head the Chicago modeling workshop are expressed in his book, *Vision in Motion*:

The new sculpture emerging from the industrial technologies started out with the "Médrano" by Archipenko, assembled from glass, wood and metal. Then came the constructivists' assemblies, studies in balance and motion, constructions in crystal plate glass, transparent plastics, metals and vulcanized fibers.[20]

He considered the sculptor a "splendid craftsman, with the added knowledge of a fine industrial mechanic and model maker," who has the capacity "to handle materials in the lathe, soldering, welding and other industrial processes." Archipenko, "artist-inventor" was clearly the man for the job.

Unfortunately, the New Bauhaus—and consequently Archipenko's association with it—was of short duration. In the summer of 1938 the board of its sponsoring organization, the Association of Arts and Industries, decided to discontinue the school because of administrative and financial problems. The members of the faculty, Archipenko included, signed a letter declaring their loyalty to Moholy-Nagy and their belief in the school's promising future. But it was not until early 1939 that Moholy-Nagy was able to reopen the school and, by this time, Archipenko was back in New York where he, in turn, had reopened his own school.

The effect of the brief Bauhaus experience on Archipenko is not immediately visible. The works of 1937 and 1938, exhibited at the Katharine Kuh Gallery in Chicago, continue along the lines established in California—textured polychromed figures in terra-cotta. *Walking Woman*, 1937 (cat. no. 36), is an example of this type of figure and was used by Moholy-Nagy in the revised edition of his first book, *The New Vision*, to illustrate the second stage of sculpture, the "modelled (hollowed out) block." Moholy-Nagy describes this as "small and large mass (volume) relationships of salient and sunken, positive and negative, round and angular, sharp and dull." He also credits Archipenko

71

with "the first conscious use of concaves in sculpture to replace salien-cies."[21] In addition to the formal features singled out by Moholy-Nagy, in *Walking Woman* color and texture are used symbolically and corre-spond to three successive layers that compose the figure. The outermost one, like a covering or shell, is highly textured, with an inlay of lumpy pebbles of reddish-brown clay. Next are areas in a smoother (although grainy) finish with a yellowish tinge. The innermost layer, the core, is concave and shiny, polished to a bright speckled red-orange color. This idea of the generalized exterior form shielding the delicate inner essence had appeared earlier with California works like *Standing Vertical* and *Head*.

It is tempting to see *Architectural Figure* (cat. no. 38), dated 1937 by Archipenko,[22] as the outcome of his being part of a community of art-ists under the respected banner of the Bauhaus. *Architectural Figure*, stocky, straight-edged, and constructivist in appearance, is an unex-pected departure from the stylish affectation of many of Archipenko's works of the 1930s. Some of its features, like the tilted circular slab of the shoulders over the cone-shaped upper torso, and the color used to artic-ulate geometric components, recall *Carrousel Pierrot* and *Médrano II*, products of another stimulating environment—Paris around 1913. Other features, like the centered, architectural stance and the regular black and white stripes, have no precedents in Archipenko's work. In fact, dated 1937, *Architectural Figure* has neither direct parentage nor any immediate offspring.

The work did not appear in Archipenko's 1944 exhibition at the Nie-rendorf Gallery in New York, a show intended as a kind of manifesto, including works from 1909 to 1944. The brochure printed for the occa-sion illustrated early works like *Carrousel Pierrot* and *Médrano I*, and it seems inconceivable that Archipenko would have chosen not to exhibit an advanced polychromed sculpture that he had in his possession. The first documented exhibition in which *Architectural Figure* was shown was in 1954, at the Associated American Artists Galleries, where the piece appeared in terra-cotta. That the piece was not shown until the 1950s and that Katharine Kuh, Archipenko's dealer in Chicago during the thirties and early forties and organizer of a number of exhibitions of his work, does not remember ever having seen the piece,[23] strongly sug-gests a later vintage. Dated 1950, *Architectural Figure* fits better both in Archipenko's work and in the general context of American sculpture, where, by the late 1940s, the constructivist aesthetic had entered the mainstream. Richard Lippold's wire constructions, for example, show the influence of the New Bauhaus environment of Chicago, where he had his early training as an artist.[24] In his work, as well as that of Sidney

Gordin (another Bauhaus inspired sculptor) there is the recurring motif of thin steel rods that create a striped structure in space. Archipenko used the stripe, but as a decorative surface motif, in polychromed works of the early 1950s. In *Egyptian Motif,* 1952, and *Hindu Princess,* 1954, for example, the regular stripe pattern adds a precise and machined quality to these otherwise flowing and organic pieces. The rectilinear building-block components and arched support of *Architectural Figure,* however, set it apart from Archipenko's other sculptures.

Archipenko spent the war years in New York City and Woodstock, where he had established a summer school in 1925 and owned a house and property. He was suffering from a bad back and was not very productive;[25] he held no exhibitions between 1944 and 1948. The works he made are small, rounded, smooth terra-cotta figures like *Spanish Woman,* 1942 (cat. no. 37). This piece, which won a prize in a ceramic exhibition at the Syracuse Museum of Fine Arts in 1949,[26] has a novel feature—it is not painted but is inlaid with a darker-toned clay. This is a tricky technique which consists of cutting into the leathery soft material and making sure that the second clay inserted into the cutout is of exactly the same consistency and water content. (Judging the amount of moisture in a lump of clay requires experience and great sensitivity to the material.)[27]

In the summer of 1943, Archipenko spent many months designing a fuel-efficient stove that could convert to each of five different fuels (kerosene, wood, coal, gas, and electricity) (fig. 38a-b). Inspired by his father, who had made a fortune on a smoke-purifying furnace, Archipenko tried unsuccessfully to patent and market this invention.

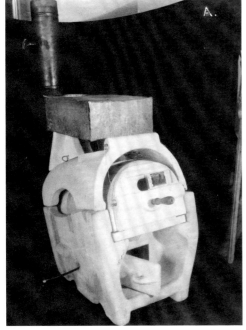
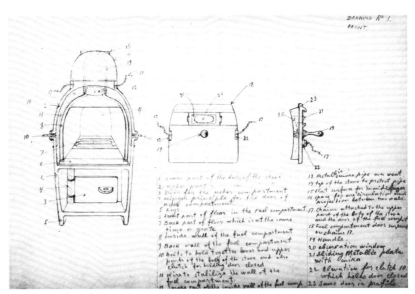

Fig. 38 a-b. Alexander Archipenko, Stove design, 1943, drawing and model.

In 1946 Archipenko was invited back to Chicago for a second teaching assignment at the Chicago Bauhaus (now named the Institute of Design). Faced with an enormous enrollment of one thousand students in 1946, Moholy-Nagy had gone to New York in search of creative people for the faculty.[28] He and Archipenko got along well with each other;[29] Moholy-Nagy knew how to handle Archipenko, who was susceptible to flattery. (He once was overhead saying, ". . . but Alexander, you are a genius.")[30] This second stint in Chicago, however, was also short-lived. Moholy-Nagy died of leukemia in November 1946 and Archipenko did not return after the spring semester of 1947.[31]

Several students from the Institute of Design in Chicago attended Archipenko's school in Woodstock in the summer of 1946. The sculptor Roy Gussow, the only male in the group (Archipenko once told him he preferred female students because men argue too much), had worked with Archipenko on a commission in Chicago and served as his assistant that summer. Gussow, his wife Mary (they met at Archipenko's school in Woodstock), and the artist Lenore Tawney all remember a summer of hard work and jovial good times.[32] They describe Archipenko as understanding, sympathetic, and a good teacher. Both Tawney and Gussow indicate, however, that the students who profited most from Archipenko's teaching were those who agreed with him; he was not overbearing, but he encouraged students who showed an inclination to work in his style. He was emotional, instinctive, and very sensitive to criticism of his work. He also loved parties, drank vodka like water, and was a great cook. "If you don't like garlic," he often said, "you can't understand modern art." He enjoyed music and could improvise at the piano. He never spoke about contemporary art and had little to do with local Woodstock artists. He was hard-working, dedicated, and very absorbed in his work. In retrospect, Tawney remembers feeling that she had to leave Archipenko's tutelage in order to find her own way, but years later, was surprised to realize that her "woven forms," the tall, vertical weavings she began to make in the 1960s, reminded her of some of Archipenko's sculptures. Gussow, noted for his abstract works in polished stainless steel, stresses that Archipenko was a careful and precise technician who was seriously concerned with the processes and the discipline of sculpture-making. The essential feature of Archipenko's art, according to Gussow, was purity of form achieved through gradual refinement and the elimination of redundancies.

A direct legacy of the Chicago Bauhaus experience seems to have been Archipenko's work with plastics and light. He began to experiment with transparency in 1947 after leaving the school, where plastic was an important material in the curriculum. Unlike Moholy-Nagy who bent and folded Plexiglas sheets heated in the kitchen stove,[33] Archipenko carved plastic with a machine of his own invention.[34] By means of a system of illumination within the transparent material, which he devised by building a light source into the base, he was able, as he described it, "to sculpt light."[35] In 1955 he wrote in a catalogue: "This area of expression has great and varied possibilities. It doesn't belong to the art of today or tomorrow, but embodies timeless spiritual truths produced by a new material and light."[36] *Ascension*, 1950 (cat. no. 39), is representative of the predominantly mystical character of Archipenko's works in plastic (two others are titled *Religious Motif*, 1948, and *Spirit*, 1957). Tall, slender vertical forms with open spaces and concavities, they recall *Standing Vertical*, 1935, in their general configuration. But transparent and glowing with their own light, they become disembodied symbols, phantoms from some mysterious, otherworldly realm.

Between 1935 and 1944 Archipenko became involved in an acrimonious dispute with Alfred H. Barr of the Museum of Modern Art in New York.[37] Published here for the first time, the content of the letters they exchanged focuses on two important issues that have clouded Archipenko's career and reputation: replication and antedating.

It began in December 1935, when Barr wrote to Archipenko in Hollywood, inviting him to participate in the exhibition *Cubism and Abstract Art*, scheduled to open in early March 1936. Barr's letter (24 December 1935) lists by title several early works that he is interested in showing. Archipenko answers (8 January 1936) that most of his early works are in European collections but adds that "by some kind of coincidence I expect at the beginning of February a collection of some of my pre-war work, arriving in Los Angeles from the Orient." He encloses photographs and lists four pieces in terra-cotta with measurements. In the correspondence that follows Barr settles on five sculptures and questions Archipenko on the 1909 date of one of them (*Hero*);[38] Archipenko agrees to send the sculptures Barr has requested and in a letter dated 21 January 1936 states, "About the dates of my works I am very sure they are correct." Sometime in late January or early February Archipenko sends Barr a cable (undated): "WORKS HAVE ARRIVED NEED TO BE REPAIRED STOP ON ELEVENTH WILL SEND THEM TO YOU STOP HERO WAS MADE IN 1910 NOT 1909 STOP SORRY FOR CONFUSION." Then, on 17 February 1936, Archipenko writes:

I am sure that by now my work has already arrived in New York. From these works only the "sculpto-painting" is the *only one existing original example. The others are the replicas of the old statues.* All the first original pieces are in private collections. Those which I have sent you are also originals because every one was sculpted individually and was not reproduced from a mold. (italics added)

And he ends the letter with:

I deeply regret that I will not be able to see this exhibition. I believe that through this show many things will be adjusted for myself *in point of view of the historical truth: that I was the originator of certain ideas and researches in modern sculpture* and I am very grateful to you that you have invited me to this show. (italics added)

The last minute pressures of the exhibition must have been formidable because Archipenko's information about the replicas either did not register with Barr, or he chose not to act on it. Moreover, Barr did not react when he saw the terra-cottas themselves, although they must have looked new. The works were exhibited as planned and the terra-cottas are listed in the catalogue with their original dates (1910–1915). Four works by Archipenko—more by him than by any other sculptor—are illustrated in the catalogue in a double-page spread. In his short essay Barr summarizes Archipenko's sculptural innovations. He acknowledges that Archipenko was "the first to work seriously and consistently at the problem of Cubist sculpture" by substituting voids for solids, by introducing color into sculpture, and by creating mixed-media constructions. He singles out *Boxing* as Archipenko's "most abstract work and his most powerful" and comments that it has no trace of "the mannered prettiness" of the later work.[39]

After the opening of the show on 2 March 1936 there was correspondence between Barr and Archipenko regarding the tour of the exhibition and a letter from Archipenko (25 March 1936) asking about the possibility of a one man show "of completely new works" at the Museum of Modern Art in early 1937. Barr's reply is negative (6 April 1936); he states that the exhibition schedule for 1937 is complete and does not leave the matter open for further discussion.

Seen in retrospect, when Archipenko received Barr's invitation in late 1935, he had been in the United States for twelve years. His early hopes for quick success in this country had all but vanished. He supported himself mainly by teaching and lecturing and through occasional commissions from Ukrainian organizations for monuments to national heroes.[40] Now he had the opportunity to participate in a major historic exhibition in an important museum, but he lacked the examples of early work that Barr specifically wanted.

Archipenko's decision to send replicas to Barr's exhibition is understandable from the point of view of a sculptor trained in the early twentieth century. He was accustomed to the practices of the nineteenth century with its traditions of multiple casts and sculpture "factories" like that of Rodin. It appears that he did not see a considerable difference between bronze casts made over a period of time from an original mold and an artist's reuse or repetition of an idea years after its original conception. In fact, he implies that the latter method is preferable when he states (17 February 1936) that the pieces he sent were "originals" because they were "sculpted individually and not reproduced from a mold." The originality he refers to is in the process of making the sculpture, not in the birth of the idea in the artist's mind. This view differs from the generally shared belief in the importance of the initial creative spark and in the unique urgency of the act of creation itself. Yet, it is entirely possible for an artist to return to an idea and reuse it repeatedly. Brancusi is a good example, and no one has ever found fault with this practice of his. Quite the contrary, we marvel at his patient, dedicated, almost obsessive return to certain forms for repeated revision and refinement, clearly traceable from the sequence of dates.

With Archipenko, the case is different; for the pieces he sent to New York in 1936 he used the term "replica," meaning "facsimile" or "duplicate," and he did not hesitate to give these California replicas the dates of the originals. But, in effect, they were not replicas—since the originals were not available, Archipenko could not copy them exactly. Based on memory and photographs, the remakes inevitably differ somewhat from the originals and are more accurately described as "versions," a term Archipenko himself later adopted.[41] He spells out his position on this issue in his book from 1960:

Sometimes I sculpt a new version of the same statue after a considerable time has elapsed. Of course, in modelling the same problem the forms are not as mathematically exact as if they were cast from the same mold. However, in all versions I prefer to keep the date of the first, since I want to conserve the chronology of the idea. The particular stylistic and creative approach I use equally in all versions unless changes are purposely made.[42]

Archipenko later remade about thirty early works from photographs and from memory. These resulted in bronze editions, many of which were begun in the mid-1950s. In some cases there is more than one edition of a work, and sometimes there are editions of the same sculpture in different sizes or in different materials. In every case the works were assigned the dates of their original creation.[43]

The critical issue with Archipenko is dating, both dating later versions as if they were the originals, as well as antedating other works.[44]

The actual controversy with Barr arose in 1943–1944 over this question of dating. That the terra-cottas sent by Archipenko to the Museum of Modern Art in 1936 were only versions of originals was less of a problem than dating these works in general. Following a meeting in New York sometime in early 1943, Archipenko invites Barr to visit his studio. In the course of two visits (alluded to in the correspondence) Barr examines catalogues, photographs, and scrapbooks, and raises certain questions about dating. After the second visit, Archipenko tries to reach Barr by phone but only speaks to Barr's wife. On 9 April 1943 Barr writes Archipenko that he is distressed by his wife's report of her conversation with him. He says he cannot understand why Archipenko has taken offense and hopes he will be willing to help clarify some problems of chronology and stylistic development. He refers to several works which were assigned three or four different dates by others and by Archipenko, where he himself was, at times, uncertain. A long exchange of letters follows. Archipenko becomes defensive and insists that his historical position was established long ago and declares his determination to defend his art against any attempt to harm it. Barr assures Archipenko that there is no conspiracy to undermine his position and that his motive is to discover "the exact truth." He argues that his decision to include six of Archipenko's works in the 1936 exhibition was proof of his recognition of Archipenko's importance.[45] In one of several long bitter letters (22 December 1943), Archipenko writes, ". . . if 20 years were not enough for you and the Museum of Modern Art to learn the exact truth about my work then please don't interfere now and keep your hands off my Art."

Barr had noted inconsistencies in the dating of *Hero* and *Walking Woman*, among others. For *Hero* Archipenko had at first supplied the date 1909 and then changed it to 1910. In reviewing the early publications Barr found either 1912 or 1913 as the date given for *Hero*. For *Walking Woman* Archipenko gave the date 1912, stating that the dates 1918 and 1919 given in early publications were wrong. Barr tentatively concluded that *Hero* should be dated 1912–1913 and *Walking Woman*, 1918–1919.[46] Despite Barr's polite and conciliatory tone, Archipenko's letters become increasingly shrill and accusatory. He could have dropped the whole affair but instead seemed to want a scandal. In the spring of 1944 he brought the matter into the public eye by issuing printed postcards announcing the forthcoming publication (unrealized) of an illustrated text in six languages titled "Why I request to remove my work from the Museum of Modern Art."

If in 1936 Archipenko already suspected that he would never regain the position he had held in the early 1920s, by 1943/1944, in his mid-fifties, he saw no recourse but to insistently mine the past. The late thirties and forties were a low period in Archipenko's life; his offer to show new work at the Museum of Modern Art in 1937 had been firmly declined. He seems to have been overly conscious of his historical position and, at the same time, naive in his disregard for the value ascribed by art historians to documents and to stylistic coherence both within an artist's work and in the broader context of the period in general. Archipenko failed to see, for example, that his 1912 dating of *Walking Woman* made it a disturbing anomaly, but that correctly dated 1918–1919 it fit comfortably between his early open-space figures of 1914–1915 and the late cubist works of 1920. Pushing the date of *Walking Woman* forward by six years (from 1912 to 1918) of course detracts from the innovative character of this particular work, but its most important feature, the large-scale substitution of voids for solids already appears, albeit expressed more cautiously, in firmly dated earlier works of 1914 and 1915 (for example, cat. nos. 16 and 19). Insecure and unrecognized in the present, Archipenko overestimated and overplayed the past.

It was also in 1944 that the question of the terra-cottas of 1936 finally surfaced. In January Archipenko held an exhibition at the Nierendorf Gallery. Advertised as his fiftieth one-man exhibition in the United States, it appears to have been staged by Archipenko to demonstrate the chronology of his innovations in modern sculpture, and featured works from 1909 to 1944. Included were two of the *Cubism and Modern Art* terra-cottas, this time labeled by Archipenko as "1935 replicas." After viewing the exhibition, Barr reproached Archipenko (letter dated 17 May 1944) for having sent him replicas of early works but later (27 May 1944) offered him "partial apology," when, on rereading the 1936 correspondence, he discovered that Archipenko had acknowledged that he was sending replicas. Although Archipenko had not made clear that they were recently-made replicas, and had earlier even written that he was expecting a shipment of "pre-war work" from the Orient, his description of the sculpture as "the replicas of the *old* statues" (italics added), should have given Barr pause.

Along with the long dispute with Alfred Barr, the appearance of Jacques Lipchitz in New York in 1941 also seems to have upset Archipenko at this time. As a refugee from the Nazis, Lipchitz was given a warm welcome, and the influential Curt Valentin became his dealer. Soon after his arrival, the Museum of Modern Art was instrumental in getting him an important sculpture commission for the Ministry of Education in Rio de Janeiro.[47] Archipenko's repeated allusions to "an accomplice," "a protégé," and "a member of the School of Paris," in his letters to Barr, no doubt refer to Lipchitz. In 1954 Lipchitz was given what the controversy with Barr had completely ruled out for Archipenko—a retrospective at the Museum of Modern Art.[48]

The decade of the 1950s and the years preceding Archipenko's death in 1964 were, even by his energetic standards, a period of frenetic activity. He taught at the University of Missouri, Kansas City (where he was commissioned to make two identical statues of *Iron Figure,* 1951, for the entrance of the campus), the Carmel Institute of Art in California, the University of Oregon, the University of Washington, Seattle, the University of Delaware, and the University of British Columbia, Vancouver. In fourteen years he had about forty exhibitions throughout the United States, as well as in Central and South America (Guatemala City and São Paulo, Brazil). He made a quantity of new sculptures in these years, but he also remade many early works for inclusion in several retrospective-style exhibitions he organized himself. For the first time in thirty years, Archipenko returned to the scene of his early successes and held a series of exhibitions in Europe. These activities, including his work on a large illustrated volume of his life's work, can only be seen as a concerted, last-ditch attempt to revive his reputation and capitalize on the improved postwar economy in this country and in Europe.

The first of the self-promoting exhibitions, held in New York in 1954 at the Associated American Artists Galleries, was so large that it had to be shown in two installments. It included eighty-nine sculptures from the years 1909 to 1954, plus drawings, paintings, and prints, totaling 163 works. In the preface of the catalogue Archipenko stressed his innovative use of new materials and the spiritual content of his work: "The creative essence of my philosophy lies in the phenomena of the immaterial, spiritual rudiments which evolve into diverse forms to become a symbolic object." He also made the following comment with regard to early works:

Unfortunately many originals cannot be exhibited because they are scattered throughout the world and the difficulties of bringing them together for exhibition are insurmountable. A number of works are replicas of old originals owned by foreign museums and collectors.[49]

In the checklist roughly one third of the works are marked "R," meaning "Replica of sculpture in foreign and American collections." But this designation, ostensibly provided for clarification, is used ambiguously. It appears next to early works that were remade in the United States from photographs and from memory without the benefit of the original (which had remained in Europe), as well as next to later American works of which there are several casts, sometimes of different materials but made from an original presumably still in the artist's possession. In the latter case, all casts are justifiably given the same date. The problem with the former case, is that, although the "R" signifies a replica, the date does not show when that replica was made. As was his practice, Archipenko gave his later versions or remakes the dates of the originals.

In the new work of these years, which is virtually unknown to date, Archipenko again explored different materials and color. A curious example of his polychromed work of the fifties is *Queen*, 1954 (cat. no. 40), a wood figure enveloped in a flaring, floor-length cloak. The strictly frontal, almost symmetrical form is painted white (cowled head), red (chest), and blue (lower two-thirds of the figure). Thin white bands outline the areas of color and bisect the figure from the chest down to the tip of the wedge-shaped base. A blue outline creates a small featureless face on the surface of the pointed white hood. But nothing prepares us for the shock of the rear view: the austere and dignified priestess turns out to be a hollow blue shell shielding an attenuated inner core. The slender wavy interior is painted a garish yellow and above is a large bulbous head of the same color. The unsettling incongruity of the two views—cool reserve in front, swelling viscera in back—has no precedent or sequel in Archipenko's work and can perhaps be seen as a belated response to surrealism.

Also surrealist in character but more typical of the polychromed works of the 1950s is *Figure*, 1957 (cat. no. 41), of painted terra-cotta. It is composed of six separate biomorphically-shaped pieces painted in contrasting but muted colors—dirty white, gold-speckled charcoal, and reddish and yellowish earth tones. Some individual parts interlock and rest on top of each other to form an armless humanoid. While modeled organic forms derived from surrealism are new to Archipenko, the additive process of piling up disparate parts can already be seen in the sculpto-paintings and sculptures of the cubist period (for example, *Seated Woman*, 1920 [cat. no. 29]). In *Figure*, and frequently in his late work, Archipenko relinquished the contrapposto that formerly pervaded his figural imagery in favor of a centered, symmetrical form; instead of being beguiling and feminine, his figures become generalized hieratic symbols or totems. The move from the formalist concerns of the early works to what Archipenko referred to as the "spiritual" content of his work is expressed in the following statement in his 1960 book:

Sculpture must have a significance beyond its form to become a symbol and produce association and relativity fixed by stylistic transformations. This sublimates sculpture into the metaphysical realm. This is the mission of art.[50]

Archipenko's European comeback began in earnest in 1955 (fig. 39).[51] It is no coincidence that it took the form of a touring exhibition of several German cities (as in 1921) and that the introduction of the catalogue was by Erich Wiese, author of one of the German monographs on

Fig. 39. Archipenko exhibition, Kunstmuseum Düsseldorf, 1955–1956.

Archipenko of the 1920s. Wiese's essay follows the encomiums of the 1920s (including the often repeated equation of Archipenko being to modern sculpture what Picasso is to modern painting), and makes only brief mention of the works of the American years. Of the fifty works shown, about half were from the European years. Some of the pieces from 1910 to 1920 were designated as "replicas," and a group of about ten were marked "Bln. A." These were said to be works that had been left behind in the Berlin studio when Archipenko left for the United States in 1923. The remainder consisted of sculpture from the 1930s through the 1950s, including examples of illuminated plastic sculpture. Paintings, drawings, and prints were also included.

The combination was repeated in 1960 in another German traveling exhibition with Wiese again authoring the catalogue preface. This one began in Hagen, the site of Archipenko's first museum exhibition in 1912/1913, in the museum named after his early benefactor, Karl-Ernst Osthaus.[52] In this catalogue one notes two significant changes: the "R" designation is dropped and all the prewar works appear in bronze rather than in terra-cotta or hydrostone, as had been the case for the "replicas" in the exhibition of the 1950s. Bronze, of course, is a much more costly material; its appearance may be explained by the fact that, by this time, Archipenko had some regular income from sales through his New York dealer, Klaus Perls.

When Perls took on Archipenko in 1957 he encouraged him to start casting properly-numbered bronze editions of his sculptures. Perls has stated his belief that an artist has the right to do whatever he pleases with his own work and that as long as the artist himself remains involved with the work, its historical value does not change. Consequently, whether a bronze edition derives from the original model or a later version of it, did not concern Perls any more than it did Archipenko. Regarding the dating, Perls has expressed the opinion that the dealer's only task is to promote and sell the work, and that dating and everything else concerning the creation of the work are entirely the responsibility of the artist himself.[53]

The retrieval in 1960 of a small group of early plasters further complicates the issue of Archipenko's bronze editions. In the summer of 1960, while in Paris with his second wife, Frances Gray (Angelica had died in 1957), Archipenko heard that some of his works had recently been seen in the south of France. Following up on this lead, he was able to contact Jean Verdier and his Russian wife, Zeneide Kramaroff (an ex-mistress of Archipenko), who had since 1921 stored a number of early Archipenko sculptures in Cannes. In the correspondence that followed, Verdier listed the works they had in storage and, at Archipenko's request, made arrangements for their shipment to New York in October 1960. Although no inventory was made of the works sent, and whatever shipping or customs documents that may have existed have not survived, the contents of the Cannes shipment—eight plasters—has been firmly established.[54] All eight plasters were subsequently cast in bronze editions started by Archipenko. Frances Gray recalls that although her husband suspected that the Verdiers had kept some works behind, he did not want to press them.[55] The sculpto-painting *Woman with Fan II* (cat. no. 21), for example, and several other sculptures and works on paper by Archipenko were subsequently acquired by Joseph H. Hirshhorn directly from Cannes. They are now in the Hirshhorn Museum in Washington.

In his Perls Galleries debut in 1957, Archipenko showed recent polychromed sculpture and eight new sculpto-paintings (the first of this medium to be made in over thirty years). These incorporated mother-of-pearl, formica, and bakelite. For its sheer size, the most ambitious was *Cleopatra*, 1957 (cat. no. 42), a seven-foot-long horizontal panel. Initially titled *Repose*, it shows an abstracted female whose partial reflection is painted on a framed "mirror" attached to the panel in the center. (The photograph in the Perls catalogue shows that the "mirror" was originally oblong and projected above the frame of the sculpto-painting.)

The panel consists of assorted swelling and swaying amoeba shapes, some painted, some in flat relief. The parts that make up the figure are enclosed within a raised frame and painted reddish-brown, cream, and yellow. A brown, wood-grained area may represent a chaise-longue with satiny blue upholstery above. Between the head of the figure and the "mirror" is a trapezoidal tray to which are attached a real string of coral beads, a bracelet, and a small mound of pink crystals. Despite the familiar subject matter—woman before mirror—and the typical materials, shapes, and textures of a commonplace interior of the 1950s, there is something nightmarish and menacing in the organic bulge of the silver-blue upholstery, the gooey swirls of paint in the wood-grain finish, and the bludgeon-shaped head with its reptilian eye.

Archipenko's work of the fifties, of which *Cleopatra* is an exemplar, has recently awakened new critical interest. For the critics who grew up during this time, these works have caused a sense of nostalgia. The critics are thrilled to discover that certain hitherto neglected work of the 1950s seems to foreshadow trends in today's art: new art is said to change the perception of old art, and stylistic similarity between new and old art is used as grounds for mutual validation.[56] (Adherents to this approach pay little heed to the fact that the ebb-and-flow of fashion and art historical revisionism is predictable and commercially induced, and that shared stylistic characteristics do not in themselves tell us anything about the respective merits of either period style. It might be more revealing to look at the social, political, and economic reasons for our positive responses in the 1980s to the style of the 1950s.)

The book, *Archipenko, Fifty Creative Years, 1908–1958,* "by Alexander Archipenko and Fifty Art Historians," was published in 1960 by Tekhne Publications, a company Archipenko started for this purpose. Numerous complimentary copies were sent out to museums, libraries, and individuals (including President and Mrs. John F. Kennedy at the White House). The large format hardcover book has 292 illustrated works, of which thirty are in color. It is by far the most complete source of illustrations of Archipenko's sculpture.[57] The text consists of a series of short essays on aesthetics and pronouncements on the philosophy of art and creativity, as well as discussions on certain aspects of the work. These are peppered with references to the writings of critics and art historians, which are reprinted in the appendix to document Archipenko's assertions. The text provides little factual information, although the appendix includes a brief biographical chronology, long lists of exhibitions, teaching positions, and owners of works, as well as a bibliography. The considerable effort of assembling all this material and recording it on his own terms was certainly worthwhile from Archipenko's point of view. Despite the book's poor graphic design, its dating errors, and the fact that it is difficult to use (there is no index of illustrations, which are not grouped chronologically but by a system that is not made quite clear to the reader), the book is still the most comprehensive, read-

Fig. 40. Alexander Archipenko, *Queen of Sheba* (1961), bronze, 65 (165) h., Courtesy Zabriskie Gallery, New York.

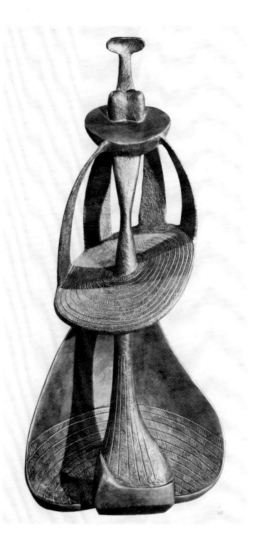

ily available, and frequently cited reference on the artist.

Despite failing health Archipenko continued to work with great vitality to the very end of his life. He prepared the following exhibitions for 1962 and 1963: a large retrospective at the Winnipeg Art Gallery (he never had a major museum exhibition in this country in his lifetime); a selection of drawings and watercolors at the Kunsthalle Mannheim; bronzes at Perls (including casts of the Cannes plasters); work from all periods at galleries in Düsseldorf and St. Gallen, Switzerland; exhibitions in Rome and Milan in 1963; and finally, a show at Galerie Stangl, Munich. Shortly after the opening of this last exhibition, Archipenko died of heart failure in New York on 26 February 1964.

Bronze was the featured medium of choice in the exhibitions of the 1960s, both for early and late work. Among the latter there are some that show an increase in scale that parallels a general trend in sculpture in the 1950s. Among the late bronzes, *Queen of Sheba*, 1961 (fig. 40), is sixty-

Fig. 41. Alexander Archipenko working on *King Solomon*, 1963.

six inches in height and *King Solomon*, 1963, Archipenko's last sculpture, was finally to have been sixty feet high. The painted plaster (cat. no. 43 and fig. 41) is the model for the colossal black and white marble which was never executed.[58] Thematically related—the Old Testament account of the Queen of Sheba's famous visit to Solomon—the two pieces can be considered complementary, the first consisting of rounded, enveloping forms (female), the other composed of pointed, thrusting elements (male). They are also examples of the two stylistic extremes of Archipenko's long career: *Queen of Sheba* represents the predominantly organic forms of the late surrealist-inspired works, while *King Solomon* looks back fifty years to Archipenko's sculpture of the cubist period. The interlocking flat wedges that aggressively invade space and the sliced and chopped angular forms of *King Solomon* were prefigured in *Boxing*, 1914 (cat. no. 14), for example. It is poignant and perhaps a little sad that Archipenko's monumental last work should so vividly invoke his period of early creativity. With this last work Archipenko had come full circle.

Notes

My sincere thanks to my good friend and colleague, Laurence Homolka, for his thorough reading of this manuscript and for his many valuable suggestions. I am grateful as well to Frances Archipenko Gray who was, once again, always readily available and prompt in responding to my numerous requests. Katherine Kuh, Lenore Tawney, Mary and Roy Gussow, Rhys Caparn, and Johannes Steel are due special thanks for kindly sharing with me recollections of their personal experiences with Archipenko. From the many others who helped me, I would like to single out Judith Zilczer, historian, Hirshhorn Museum and Sculpture Garden, Colleen Hennessey, archives assistant, Archives of American Art, and Irina Subotić, curator, Belgrade Museum. Finally, among the members of the impeccable and courteous staff at the National Gallery of Art, I would especially like to thank Jack Cowart, Dodge Thompson, and Debbie Shepherd for making my job as guest curator so pleasant, and Jill Steinberg for her understanding and conscientious editing of the text.

The part of this essay dealing with Archipenko's years in France is derived from my Ph.D. dissertation, *Archipenko: A Study of the Early Works, 1908–1920* (Columbia University, 1975; Garland Publishing, Inc., New York, 1977). This was a thorough examination of the sculptures of these years (close to 120 pieces) in the context of the period. Information from my comprehensive archive of early catalogues and publications, combined with careful stylistic analyses, resulted in the redating of a number of early works. My conclusions, which eliminated some disturbing inconsistencies of dating, have happily borne the test of time. While some new material has come to light in the intervening years, my chronology has not changed and forms the basis for the dating of works in this essay and catalogue.

Unless otherwise noted, translations are provided by the author.

Part I

1. Yvon Taillandier, "Conversation avec Archipenko," *XX Siècle*, n.s., XXVe année, no. 22 (Christmas 1963).
2. For a detailed account of Archipenko's contacts with the cubists, see Michaelsen 1977, 41-47.
3. Archipenko may have influenced Henri Gaudier-Brzeska, who lived nearby in Montparnasse before moving to London in 1911 (Alexander Archipenko, in an interview with Edward F. Fry in 1962). Gaudier's *Maternity*, for example, exhibited in London in 1914, is block-shaped and shows the same enveloping motherly embrace. Another work by Gaudier, *Boy and Coney*, brings to mind Archipenko's *Woman and Cat*, 1911, in the exceptional fusion of human and animal. See also Horace Brodzky, *Henri Gaudier-Brzeska (1891–1915)* (London, 1933); and Ezra Pound, *Gaudier-Brzeska, A Memoir* (New York, 1970).
4. Erich Wiese, "Alexander Archipenko," *Junge Kunst*, Band 40 (Leipzig, 1923), 4.
5. Albert E. Elsen, *The Partial Figure in Modern Sculpture* [exh. cat., Baltimore Museum of Art] (Baltimore, 1969), 20.
6. When the piece was first exhibited in Amsterdam in 1914 (De Onafhankelijken, Third International Exhibition, May–June), it was listed as "*Mère dans les rochers*"; the switch from "Mother"—early references often give the title *Woman and Child*—to "Madonna" is in keeping with the elaborate baroque appearance of the work. The title change may have occurred when the bronze edition was made from the original plaster that Archipenko had given to Léger, purchased with his dealer Klaus Perls from Nadia Léger in 1960, and subsequently donated to the Museum of Modern Art, New York.
7. John Golding, *Cubism: A History and an Analysis, 1907–1914*, rev. ed. (New York, 1968), 27-28.
8. Douglas Cooper, *The Cubist Epoch* (New York, 1971), 60-62.
9. Albert E. Elsen, *Origins of Modern Sculpture: Pioneers and Premises* (New York, 1974), 112.
10. Theodor Däubler and Iwan Goll, *Archipenko Album* (Potsdam, 1921), 15.

11. George Heard Hamilton, *Painting and Sculpture in Europe, 1880–1940*, rev. ed. (Baltimore, 1983), 271.

12. Alexander Archipenko and Fifty Art Historians, *Fifty Creative Years, 1908–1958* (New York, 1960), 55-58, pls. 169-181.

13. Jacques Lipchitz and H. H. Arnason, *My Life in Sculpture* (New York, 1972), 37.

14. Herbert Read, *Henry Moore* (New York, 1966), 90-92.

15. One-man exhibition catalogues are listed alphabetically by city in the Bibliography, under *Archipenko Exhibition Catalogues.*

16. At the Armory Show in New York Archipenko exhibited four sculptures, one of which was *Repose*, 1912 (cat. no. 5); in Budapest (Nemzetközi Posztimpreszionista Kiál-litás, Müvészház) he showed five works.

17. *Apollinaire on Art, Essays and Reviews, 1902–1918*, ed. LeRoy C. Breunig; trans. Susan Suleiman (New York, 1972), 356, 503, n. 7. This is the source for the translations of Apollinaire's reviews quoted in the present essay.

18. Gino Severini, *Tutta la vita di un pittore* (Milan, 1946), 164.

19. Däubler and Goll 1921, 13. The illustration of *Carrousel Pierrot* (fig. 6) in this volume published in 1921 is the only known early photograph of this sculpture. It does not show the large blue sphere that is now attached to the lower side of the cone of the "upper torso" of Pierrot. It appears that this photograph was taken before the sphere was added by Archipenko and that the piece was not rephotographed afterward. As he had sold it to Magnelli in 1914 (who took it with him to Florence), Archipenko must have supplied the publisher with the only photograph he had available. It seems unlikely that the sphere was added later by someone other than the artist—and there is no record of any such addition at the Guggenheim Museum (conversation with Vivian Barnett, 7 April 1986)—because Archipenko illustrated two views of *Carrousel Pierrot* in his 1960 book, both of which clearly show the large blue sphere (plates 3 and 4).

20. George Heard Hamilton and William C. Agee, *Raymond Duchamp-Villon, 1876–1918* (New York, 1967), 100. Archipenko's interest in Bergson may have derived from his contacts with the Puteaux artists.

21. Archipenko's influence on the German sculptor Rudolf Belling, whose works explore the same problem, was recognized (for example, *Dreiklang*, model 1919, cast 1950, Bayerische Staatsgemäldesammlung, Munich). See Roland Schacht, "Archipenko, Belling und Westheim," *Der Sturm*, Jahrg. 40, Heft 5 (May 1923), 76-78. Lipchitz began to explore the relation of mass and space in 1925 in his series of "transparents;" see Lipchitz and Arnason 1972, 85.

22. Béni Ferenczy, *Irás és Kép* (Budapest, 1961), 26-35.

23. *Archivi del Futurismo*, 2 vols., ed. Maria Drudi Gambillo and Teresa Fiori (Rome, 1958–1962), 246 (letter from Boccioni to Severini asking for the very latest work by Picasso and Braque being shown at Kahnweiler, dated June–July 1912). Marianne W. Martin, in *Futurist Art and Theory, 1905–1915* (London, 1968), 127, acknowledges the importance of cubist ideas for Boccioni's sculpture manifesto. See also Françoise Cachin, "Futurism in Paris, 1909–1913," *Art in America* (March–April 1974), 39-44.

24. Severini 1946, 164.

25. In *L'Intransigeant*, 21 June 1913 (Apollinaire 1972, 321).

26. See Katherine J. Michaelsen, "Early Mixed-Media Constructions," *Arts Magazine* (January 1976), 72-76; and Margit Rowell, *The Planar Dimension: Europe 1912–1932*, [exh. cat., The Solomon R. Guggenheim Museum] (New York, 1979).

27. *Guitar*, Paris, early 1912, sheet metal and wire, The Museum of Modern Art, New York. Braque's relief constructions have not survived.

28. Archipenko 1960, 46; also, Wiese 1923, 5.

29. Prague, Forty-fifth Exhibition of the Mánes Fine Arts Association, February–March 1914.

30. Archipenko 1960, caption to pl. 63.

31. Apollinaire 1972, 355. Apollinaire is wrong in speaking of more than one sculpture in various materials. The other pieces shown (*Gondolier, Carrousel Pierrot*, and *Boxing*), though painted, were made of plaster only.

32. *Vladimir Baranoff-Rossiné* [exh. cat., Musée National d'Art Moderne] (Paris,

1973). One of these constructions was made in the 1930s. See also *Russian Avant-Garde, 1908–1922* [exh. cat., Leonard Hutton Galleries] (New York, 1971), nos. 4-7.

33. One source, Ruth Olson and Abraham Chanin, *Gabo-Pevsner* (New York, 1948), 15-19, 24, and 51-53, states that Gabo met Archipenko in Paris. A very recent one, Steven Nash and Jörn Merkert, *Naum Gabo—Sixty Years of Constructivism* [exh. cat., Dallas Museum of Art] (Gerstel Verlag, Munich, 1985), 13, reports that Gabo denied ever having met Archipenko but acknowledged having seen Archipenko's work at the Salon des Indépendants.

34. Archipenko 1960, caption to pl. 193.

35. Maurice Raynal, *A. Archipenko* (Rome, 1923), 9.

36. Archipenko 1960, caption to pl. 182, gives 1913 as the date for *Head*. This is incorrect; according to Mrs. Frances Archipenko Gray the piece was made c. 1957.

37. Cynthia Jaffee McCabe, *The Golden Door, Artist-Immigrants of America, 1876–1976* [exh. cat., Hirshhorn Museum and Sculpture Garden] (Washington, 1976), 188.

38. *Le Petit Messager des Arts et des Industries d'Art*, 1 March 1915 (Apollinaire 1972, 440). Archipenko was not married until 1921. Apollinaire must be referring to a mistress (possibly Zeneide [Zena] Kramaraoff, later Verdier).

39. Archipenko 1960, 40-41.

40. As in A.M. Hammacher, *Jacques Lipchitz, His Sculpture* (New York, 1960), 30; and in Douglas Cooper, *The Cubist Epoch* (New York, 1971), 242.

41. *Alexander Archipenko (Elfte Retrospektive Ausstellung). Lyonel Feininger* [exh. cat., Kunstsalon Ludwig Schames] (Frankfurt, 1922), no pagination.

42. Archipenko 1960, 40-41, 43.

43. Apollinaire makes numerous references to De Chirico in his Salon reviews in these years (see Apollinaire 1972).

44. Hannah Höch's *Cut with a Kitchen Knife*, 1919 (Nationalgalerie, Staatliche Museen Berlin) is an early example.

45. Hans Hildebrandt, *Alexander Archipenko* (Berlin, 1923), 15.

46. Letter to Marcel Duchamp, 16 January 1921, The Société Anonyme Collection, Collection of American Literature, Beinecke Rare Book and Manuscript Library, Yale University.

47. For a detailed discussion of the collectors Falk and Goeritz, see Nehama Guralnik's essay in this catalogue.

48. Irina Subotić, "Une Nouvelle Acquisition du Musée National de Belgrade: *Deux Femmes* d'Alexandre Archipenko. Archipenko en Yougoslavie," *Recueil du Musée National*, XI-2 Histoire de l'Art, Musée National (Belgrade, 1982), 232.

49. Rowell 1979, 59; and Joan Marter, in *Archipenko: Drawings, Reliefs and Constructions* [exh. cat., Edith C. Blum Institute, Bard College] (Annandale-on-Hudson, N.Y., 1985), 17.

50. See, for example, Rodin's use of the vase as an analogy for the female figure in several drawings (Albert E. Elsen and J. Kirk Varnedoe, *The Drawings of Rodin* [New York, 1972], 126-127, figs. 80 and 96).

51. Archipenko, in a letter to Marcel Duchamp, 7 November 1920, The Société Anonyme Collection.

52. Archipenko, in an interview with Edward F. Fry in 1962.

53. *Yellow Bird* was shown in the Salon des Indépendants, Paris 1920 (see Sidney Geist, *Brancusi, The Sculpture and Drawings* [New York, 1975], 183, no. 124).

Part II

1. Galerie d'Art des Éditions Georges Crès & Cie., Paris, 27 May–14 June 1919.

2. This information comes from a mimeographed sheet setting forth the aims and by-laws of the association, which Archipenko sent to Katherine S. Dreier in his letter of 25 May 1920 (The Société Anonyme Collection).

3. See Bibliography, *Archipenko Exhibition Catalogues*.

4. Correspondence and materials relating to Archipenko's activities with the Société Anonyme are from The Société Anonyme Collection.

5. See note 6 below.

6. The four drawings are: *Composition*, 1920, gouache, watercolor, and pencil on paper, 12⁷/₁₆ x 9⁷/₁₆ in., Hirshhorn Museum and Sculpture Garden, Smithsonian Institution, Washington; *Seated Woman*, 1920, gouache on paper, 12¹/₁₆ x 9½, Collection of the Tel Aviv Museum, Gift of the Goeritz Family, London; *Figure Seated at a Table*, c. 1920, gouache, 11⁷/₈ x 8¾, The Société Anonyme and the Dreier Bequest at Yale University (bought by Katherine S. Dreier, probably for $100); and *Seated Woman*, 1920, watercolor, 11¾ x 8½, Collection Mr. Gerhard von Hessart, New York.

7. Probably *Figure (Sketch for a Construction)*, c. 1918–1919, gouache on cream-colored wove paper, 11 x 8½, The Société Anonyme and the Dreier Bequest at Yale University.

8. Iwan Goll, "Archipenko," *Horizont*, no. 26 (Vienna, 1921), no pagination; and Iwan Goll, "Archipenko," *Ma—Aktivista Folyóirat* VI, no. 6 (Vienna, 25 April 1921), 71-78.

9. Letter to Iván Hevesy, 26 May 1921, Berlin, Charlottenburg (in Krisztina Passuth, *László Moholy-Nagy* [New York, 1985], 389).

10. Raynal 1923, 12.

11. Subotić, 1982, 233; and Irina Subotić, "Die Zeitschrift 'Zenit' und die Erscheinung des Konstruktivismus," in *Jugoslavischer Konstruktivismus, 1921–1981* (Ratingen, 1983), 12-20.

12. Däubler and Goll 1921, 13.

13. Däubler and Goll 1921, 10; also Fannina W. Halle, "Kandinsky, Archipenko, Chagall," *Die Bildende Künste*, vol. 11/12 (1921), 182.

14. Schacht, translation from Archipenko 1960, 72, no. 7.

15. *The Letters and Diaries of Oskar Schlemmer*, sel. and ed. Tut Schlemmer, trans. Krishna Winston (Middletown, Conn., 1972), 27, 69, 166. My thanks to the late Mr. Andreas Weininger for bringing to my attention Schlemmer's interest in Archipenko.

16. *Dresdener Sezession 1919–1923* [exh. cat., Galleria del Levante] (Munich, 1977), texts by Fritz Löffler and Joachim Heusinger v. Waldegg. See also Stephanie Barron, *German Expressionist Sculpture* [exh. cat., Los Angeles County Museum of Art] (Chicago, 1984).

17. My thanks to Laurence Homolka for the information on Bruno Schnitz.

18. Conversation with Katharine Kuh, 26 November and 9 December 1985. Kuh was Archipenko's dealer in Chicago in the 1930s and early 1940s; her recollections vividly brought to life both Archipenko and his wife.

19. Conversation with Lenore Tawney, New York, 10 January 1986. Tawney was Archipenko's student at the Institute of Design in 1946 and in Woodstock in the summer of that same year. She and another student, Roy Gussow (conversation, New York, 7 February 1986) confirmed the aristocrat/peasant contrast between husband and wife. Tawney also recalled that Angelica often teased her husband for being terrified of horses.

20. Examples are works by Bernhard Hoetger, Fritz Klimsch, Ernst Wenck, Theodor Georgii, Fritz Behn, and others.

21. Hans Hildebrandt, *Die Kunst des XIX und XX Jahrhunderts* (Potsdam, 1924), 441-442.

22. Carl Einstein, *Die Kunst des XX Jahrhunderts* (Berlin, 1926), 170-174.

Part III

1. *Exhibition of Russian Painting and Sculpture*, Brooklyn Museum, 23 January–4 March 1923. The six pieces by Archipenko in this exhibition were the sculpto-paintings that remained in the United States after his Société Anonyme exhibition in 1921.

2. *International Exhibition of Modern Art*, Brooklyn Museum, November–December 1926.

3. Galka Scheyer Papers, Archives of American Art, Smithsonian Institution, Washington.

4. *The Blue Four, Feininger, Jawlensky, Kandinsky, Paul Klee* [exh. cat., Leonard Hutton Galleries] (New York, 1984); foreword by Peg Weiss, 7-12.

5. Beginning in 1926 Archipenko had printed stationery that read: "Ecole Beaux Arts/A. Archipenko/44 West 57 Street/Sculpture/Painting/Drawing/and Institute for Studies in Theory of Art." A new letterhead in 1927 added to the subjects taught at the school "Ceramic, mosaic and work in marble and wood." The sculptress Rhys Caparn studied with Archipenko from 1931 to 1933. Caparn spoke warmly of Archipenko as a marvelous teacher who gave of himself and was like a father to his students (in conversation with author, 20 January 1986).

6. *The Société Anonyme and the Dreier Bequest at Yale University. A Catalogue Raisonne*, ed. Robert L. Herbert, Eleanor S. Apter, and Elise K. Kenney (New Haven and London), 1984. A selection of one hundred works from the Société Anonyme-organized *International Exhibition of Modern Art* at the Brooklyn Museum in 1926 was shown at the Anderson Galleries in January 1927 before traveling to Buffalo and Toronto.

7. Stanley Casson, *XXth Century Sculptors* (London, 1930), 61-69.

8. Patent #1,626,496 for "Apparatus for Displaying Changeable Pictures," and #1,626,497 for "Method for Decorating Changeable Display Apparatus," dated Washington, 26 April 1927. See Archipenko 1960, pls. 290-292.

9. Linda Dalrymple Henderson, *The Fourth Dimension and Non-Euclidian Geometry in Modern Art* (Princeton, 1983), 358.

10. Henderson 1983, 359.

11. Coining trade names, establishing theories, and issuing manifestos about the incorporation of the machine into art are also symptomatic of the period. A little-known example that has interesting parallels with Archipenko's invention is Henryk Berlewi's Mechano-Faktura manifesto published in *Der Sturm* in 1924. In the manifesto Berlewi proposed to free modern painting from subjectivity and illusion by mechanical schematization of technique and texture. Like Archipenko, Berlewi insists that automation would not affect the creative process itself, but that instead, mechanization of the process of painting would provide greater freedom and increase the possibilities of invention. Berlewi knew Archipenko's work and mentions his sculpto-painting in the manifesto. The two men may even have met, either in Paris in 1911/1912, or a decade later in Berlin where both were in the circle of Der Sturm. Berlewi also adapted his Mechano-Faktura theory to commercial use when, upon returning to Poland, he established an advertising firm which he named Mechano-Reklama. See *Henryk Berlewi (1894–1967)* [exh. cat. with translation of Mechano-Faktura manifesto] (La Boétie, Inc., New York, 1978).

12. As reported by Mrs. Frances Archipenko Gray, 14 November 1985. The U.S. Patent Office at one time required the deposit of prototype-models, but this practice was discontinued several years before Archipenko's patents were issued.

13. Archipenko 1960, 65-66.

14. *Société Anonyme* 1984, 15.

15. "Archipenko to Show at Saks," *The Art News* 27 (14 September 1929), 10.

16. Archipenko 1960, list of exhibitions, 91-94.

17. As reported by the sculptor Roy Gussow, a student of Archipenko's, on 7 February 1986.

18. Hans M. Wingler, *The Bauhaus, Weimar, Dessau, Berlin, Chicago* (Cambridge, Mass. and London, 1978), 192-198, 577, 581.

19. László Moholy-Nagy, *The New Vision and Abstract of an Artist* (New York, 1946), 74.

20. László Moholy-Nagy, *Vision in Motion* (Chicago, 1946), 235.

21. Moholy-Nagy 1946, 43.

22. Archipenko 1960, pl. 1.

23. In conversation with author, 26 November 1985.

24. Wayne Andersen, *American Sculpture in Process: 1930/1970* (Boston, 1975), 80.

25. As reported by Mrs. Frances Archipenko Gray, 14 November 1985.

26. "Thirteenth National Ceramic Exhibition," *American Artist* (January 1949), 46-47.

27. As reported by Roy Gussow, 7 February 1986.

28. Sibyl Moholy-Nagy, *Moholy-Nagy, Experiment in Totality* (New York, 1950), 234-235.

29. According to Katharine Kuh, in conversation with author, 26 November 1985.

30. As reported by Roy Gussow, 7 February 1986.

31. Archipenko had a disagreement with Serge Chermayeff, Moholy-Nagy's successor as director of the Institute of Design. In a letter (30 January 1947, Alexander Archipenko Papers, Archives of American Art, Smithsonian Institution, Washington) informing Archipenko of his teaching assignment for the spring term, Chermayeff requests him not to introduce color to his first semester sculpture students because they "are not equipped to work intelligently with color." Archipenko was outraged at this interference in his teaching method and, violating his contract as a full-time faculty member at the Institute, placed an ad in the 16 February 1947 issue of *Herald-American* announcing the opening of his own private art school. Although the matter was temporarily patched up, Archipenko did not return to the Institute after the end of the semester.

32. Conversations with Lenore Tawney (10 January 1986) and Mr. and Mrs. Roy Gussow (7 February 1986).

33. Sibyl Moholy-Nagy 1950, 191.

34. Frances Archipenko Gray, in conversation with author, 8 September 1985.

35. Yvon Taillandier 1963, no pagination.

36. *Alexander Archipenko: Plastik, Malerei, Zeichnungen, Druckgraphik* (Düsseldorf, 1955–1956).

37. The Museum of Modern Art Archives: Alfred Barr Papers, Archives of American Art, Washington.

38. The sculptures chosen by Barr were *Hero, Walking Woman* (fig. 5), *Boxing* (cat. no. 14), *Geometric Statuette* (cat no. 16), and *Bather* (sculpto-painting) (fig. 19).

39. Alfred H. Barr, Jr., *Cubism and Abstract Art* (New York, 1936), 103-104, 204, figs. 92-95.

40. A portrait of the poet Taras Shewchenko, 1933, was made in several casts for various locations, including a Ukrainian garden in Cleveland for which Archipenko also created statues of Vladimir the Great and Ivan Franko. Another monument to poet Shashkewitch was made for Philadelphia.

41. The terra-cotta version of *Boxing* (1935), for example, is 7⅜ inches larger than the plaster exhibited at the 1914 Salon (cat. no. 14) and a second plaster cast from the same mold which Archipenko retrieved in 1960 and cast in bronze (the Museum of Modern Art). The terra-cotta version, which bears an incised inscription ("LA BOXE/C'est la musique/monumental/des volumes d'espace/et de la matière/Archipenko/Paris 1913"), was purchased from the artist c.1941 by the Peggy Guggenheim Collection, Venice (see Angelica Zander Rudenstine, *Peggy Guggenheim Collection, Venice* [New York, 1985], 54-58).

42. Archipenko 1960, caption to pl. 141.

43. In April 1974 the College Art Association of America's Board of Directors issued "A Statement on Standards for Sculptural Reproduction and Preventive Measures to Combat Unethical Casting in Bronze." Since the appearance of this widely-discussed document, there has been a gradual move toward clear disclosure of casting dates, indications as to whether a cast is lifetime or posthumous, and whether the model used for casting was the original or a later version. But regrettably, in the case of Archipenko, his own practice of assigning the date of the original idea to subsequent versions is still too frequently used.

44. Uncertainty about the dates of some of Archipenko's early works has led some authors to the unreasonable extreme of questioning the dates of all the early pieces (A. M. Hammacher, *Jacques Lipchitz*, trans. James Brockway [New York, 1975], 27, 56). Lipchitz, with whom Archipenko shared a bitter rivalry in the late years, wrote: "As to Archipenko, one has to be careful about the dating of his early Cubist pieces. I'd like to see them reproduced in some magazines before the war to be certain that they were actually made then" (Lipchitz and Arnason 1972, 16).

45. The sixth work by Archipenko, on loan from the Weyhe Gallery, was a bronze cast of *Woman Combing Her Hair*, 1915 (fig. 4). This was probably the same cast that was subsequently purchased by the Museum of Modern Art from the Weyhe Gallery.

46. My dating of these works concurs with Barr's (see *Archipenko: A Study of the Early Work*, *1908–1920* [New York, 1977], 78-81, 92-93; and "The Chronology of Archipenko's Paris Years," *Arts Magazine* [November 1976], 91-93).

47. Lipchitz and Arnason 1972, 164.

48. In 1970 the Museum of Modern Art held a small exhibition of Archipenko's works titled *Archipenko: The Parisian Years*.

49. *Archipenko, 110th Exhibition, Fifty Years Production* [exh. cat., Associated American Artists Galleries] (New York, 1954).

50. Archipenko 1960, 35.

51. Traveling exhibition, Germany, 1955–1956.

52. *Alexander Archipenko; Plastiken, 1909–1959*, Hagen (Karl-Ernst Osthaus Museum) and Münster (Freie Künstlergemeinschaft Schanze, Munster Hauptbahnhof), 1960.

53. In conversation with author, 25 September 1985 and 3 January 1986.

54. In a letter dated 29 July 1960, Verdier lists the following pieces, which were subsequently shipped to New York: *Adam and Eve*, 1909; *Mother and Child*, 1910–1911; *Woman with Cat*, 1911; *Repose*, 1912; *Boxing*, 1914; and *Danse Rouge* (renamed *Blue Dancer*), 1913–1918. Although Verdier also mentioned a sculpto-painting *Woman with Fan*, 1915, and "several small statuettes," these were not included in the shipment. Frances Gray recalls, however, that two additional works, *Seated Woman*, 1912, and *Small Reclining Figure*, 1913, were included.

55. In conversation with author, 8 September 1985.

56. Robert Rosenblum has written: ". . . as is often the case in the story of drastic shifts of taste, it is the younger artist who leads the way. The free-floating fantasies of Clemente, for example, make us see the late work of Chagall with newer, more sympathetic eyes; the see-through superpositions of realist drawings on abstract grounds in the work of Polke or Salle give the late Picabia a new lease on life; . . . and so it goes with Archipenko's *Cleopatra* too. . . . [it] has been resurrected in the work of such younger painters as Jedd Garet, who populates his New Surrealist spaces with a progeny of slickly contoured featureless humanoids that might have stemmed from Cleopatra's own loins." See "Notes on Archipenko's *Cleopatra*," in *Archipenko: Drawings, Reliefs and Constructions* [exh. cat., Edith C. Blum Art Institute, Bard College Center] (Annandale-on-Hudson, N.Y., 1985), 9-10. In a recent article in *The New Criterion*, Jed Perl summarizes the phenomenon: "Fifties nostalgia is almost the lingua franca of the contemporary art scene" (January 1986, 22). Archipenko's works of the 1950s have been featured in exhibitions at Zabriskie Gallery in 1976 and 1979 (see Bibliography, *Archipenko Exhibition Catalogues*).

57. Sculptures which were not available at the time of publication or which have reappeared since Archipenko's death in 1964 are, of course, missing, but they are relatively few in number (see Michaelsen 1977, 20, n. 3).

58. *King Solomon* exists also in two bronze versions measuring 53 and 26½ inches.

The Erich Goeritz Collection of Works by Alexander Archipenko at the Tel Aviv Museum

History of a Collection: The Collectors S. G. Falk and Erich Goeritz

THE ERICH GOERITZ COLLECTION of works by Alexander Archipenko at the Tel Aviv Museum, comprising thirty sculptures, sculpto-paintings, paintings, and works on paper, is the largest extant collection of the artist's early works. Twenty-three pieces are part of the permanent collection and seven are on extended loan from a private collector in London. With the exception of *Sketch for Ceiling* of 1913, which was acquired in 1983, all of these early Archipenko works formed part of the collection sent by the German Jewish collector, Erich Goeritz, to Tel Aviv from Berlin in 1933 at the time of Hitler's ascent to power to ensure their survival.

When Archipenko left Europe for the United States in 1923, he left behind most of his early works from his French (1908–1921) and German (1921–1923) periods. A number of his works had already been destroyed in France and Germany during World War I.[1] Archipenko believed that several of the early plasters left in Cannes after the war were lost, until they were rediscovered in 1960. Other works were in collections in Germany where, during the 1920s, he had won greater acclaim than anywhere else. With the rise of the Fascists in Germany, Archipenko's work appeared on the lists of art declared "degenerate" by the Nazis and was subject to the widespread confiscations in which many art works were seized and destroyed.

While in America, Archipenko could not be certain as to how much of his work had survived abroad. Only in 1947 did he learn that a collection of more than thirty of his early works was safe in Tel Aviv.[2] And only in 1960 were some of the plasters rediscovered in Cannes. This may, in part, have accounted for the need he felt to recreate some of his early

OPPOSITE PAGE
Above: Fig. 1. Dizengoff House, Tel Aviv, c. 1910, home of Meir Dizengoff (first mayor of Tel Aviv), later the Tel Aviv Museum (1932).

Below: Fig. 2. Dizengoff House, Rothschild Boulevard, Tel Aviv, 1926.

works, producing duplicates and new versions of a number of them in various media, relying on photographs or upon his memory alone.

The fact that Archipenko created more than one version of the same work at long intervals made it difficult in later years to identify the original early works and determine their dates. Despite the fact that the new versions were made much later, Archipenko dated them according to the year of their original creation, the principle guiding him being a desire to mark the date on which the idea was conceived:

Sometimes I sculpt a new version of the same statue after considerable time has elapsed. Of course, in modeling the same problem the forms are not as mathematically exact as if they were cast from the same mold. However, on all versions I prefer to keep the date of the first, since I want to conserve the chronology of the idea. The particular stylistic and creative approach I use equally in all versions unless changes are purposely made.[3]

Only a few of the extant bronzes can be identified with certainty as having been cast in Europe from the original early plasters. All in all, the number of original early carved or modeled sculptures and sculptopaintings that have survived is small. Identifying Archipenko's early works and dating them precisely on the basis of bibliographical sources is also unusually difficult because of the artist's repetition and interchanging of titles, as well as inconsistencies in his datings. The works in the Tel Aviv Museum, however, are indisputably documented in the early literature, and their provenance can be reliably reconstructed.

Fig. 3. The Tel Aviv Museum, Dizengoff House, rebuilt in 1935, 14 May 1948 (Declaration of Independence).

The Archipenko Collection has been at the Tel Aviv Museum since its earliest days (the museum was founded in 1932, one year before the collection was received). Together with the museum and the city of Tel Aviv itself, the collection weathered World War II, the War of Independence, the Declaration of the State of Israel (held in 1948 at the Tel Aviv Museum, Dizengoff House), and the many wars that followed. The young museum (figs. 1–3) that was founded years before the bustling city would grow to surround it, and even before the State of Israel was established, could not always maintain the most up-to-date professional standards. Thus, for example, the humidity and change in weather conditions left their mark on the works, which subsequently required restoration. Similarly, little information concerning the documentation and provenance of the collection was recorded or preserved during this early period.

Archipenko's works were exhibited intermittently over the years with the permanent collection of the museum (figs. 4–5) and periodically in temporary exhibitions. An exchange of letters between Archipenko and the museum was initiated by the artist in 1947. On 1 July of this year Haim Gamzu assumed his post as museum director, and on the following day he wrote to the artist, proposing an exhibition of his works. Archipenko enthusiastically agreed and suggested that it focus on both his

97

early and later works. In his reply to Gamzu, he wrote that he had already had seventy-six one-man shows in various countries, and that he would be delighted to hold an exhibition in Israel, ". . . particularly since your people appreciate and own my work more than any others."[4] He added, "My sentiments and gratitude induce me to present your museum and your people with a gift, if the exhibition becomes possible. Eight years ago I created a statue of Moses (seven feet high). At the moment it is in temporary material. It must be executed in wood, which will take at least a year." He also offered to send a series of bronze, terracotta, and plastic sculpture to the exhibition. The exhibition, however, did not take place.

Restoration of the Goeritz Collection to its original state of preservation began in 1974. When Marc Scheps became museum director in 1976, he invited Donald Karshan to research and document the Archipenko Collection. Karshan carried out the first comprehensive study since 1933 in an attempt to date the works in the collection, place them stylistically within the context of the artist's oeuvre, supply bibliographical documentation, and reconstruct their provenance. Four years later, in 1980, a permanent exhibition, *Archipenko, The Early Works: 1910–1921,* was mounted by the Tel Aviv Museum (figs. 6–8). As a result of this exhibition and the accompanying catalogue, the Archipenko Collection, hitherto unknown outside Israel, became widely known internationally for the first time.

The correspondence between the museum and the Goeritz family,

Fig. 6. The present Tel Aviv Museum, inaugurated 19 April 1971.

Fig. 7. Installation of the Erich Goeritz
Collection at the Tel Aviv Museum, 1981.

preserved in the museum archives, as well as biographical information supplied by various members of the family, aided in determining the provenance of the collection from the late 1920s, when it was acquired by Erich Goeritz in Berlin.[5] Very little, however, was known about the collection prior to this time.

Only recently has it been established that the Archipenko Collection and several other works from the Goeritz Collection were formerly owned by the collector Falk, originally of Mannheim, hitherto known primarily as a Lehmbruck collector.

99

Above: Fig. 8. Installation of the Erich Goeritz Collection at the Tel Aviv Museum, 1981.

Below: Fig. 9. Alexander Archipenko, *Standing Woman/Mrs. Falk*, 1920, wax, The Tel Aviv Museum, The Erich Goeritz Collection.

Several of the works in the collection were mentioned in early literature as belonging to "G. Falk of Geneva." The collection included two portrait sculptures by Archipenko—*Double Portrait/Mr. and Mrs. Falk* (cat. no. 30), in painted plaster, and *Standing Woman/Mrs. Falk* (fig. 9), in wax. In addition to the works by Archipenko, the Goeritz Collection donated to the Tel Aviv Museum included a number of pieces by Wilhelm Lehmbruck, among them *Portrait of Mr. F.* (fig. 10) and *Portrait Statuette of Mrs. Falk (Woman in Kimono)* (fig. 11), which are now known to be portraits of Mr. Sally Falk of Mannheim and his wife, Mrs. Adèle Falk. In consultations with the Lehmbruck Museum in Duisburg and with several art historians,[6] it was suggested that George Falk of Geneva might have been a brother of the better-known collector, Sally Falk of Mannheim—Wilhelm Lehmbruck's patron and friend—who donated a large number of works to the Kunsthalle Mannheim collection.

The most recent and comprehensive study of Sally Falk was carried out by Suzanne Schiller of Heidelberg University,[7] who made use of archives in Mannheim as well as early bibliographical material. Schiller's research revealed that Sally Falk did not have a brother.[8] Due to unfortunate circumstances, he was forced to leave Mannheim and must have started a new career in Geneva under a different name—George. Thus, Lehmbruck's German patron later became the Swiss collector of Archipenko's work.

The German era in the history of the Falk Collection is more thoroughly documented today than is its Swiss period. In Germany, however, Falk's activities as a collector and his generous donations to the Kunsthalle were belatedly recognized, perhaps for the same reasons that compelled him to leave the city.

Sally Falk, the son of Felix and Ida Falk, was born in Heilbronn, Germany, in 1888. In 1899 his father set up a cotton processing plant in Neckarau, thus contributing to the massive economic surge that marked Mannheim's development as an industrial city at the turn of the century. Felix Falk died in 1914, followed two years later by his wife, so that in 1916 Sally Falk became the sole heir to the Felix Falk Company. Together with his French wife, Adèle (née Demolis), he settled in one of the more exclusive sections of Mannheim—at Mollstrasse 18, near the Kunsthalle Mannheim.[9] World War I undoubtedly played a role in pro-

Left: Fig. 10. Wilhelm Lehmbruck, *Portrait of Mr. F.*, 1915-1916, bronze, The Tel Aviv Museum, The Erich Goeritz Collection.

Right: Fig. 11. Wilhelm Lehmbruck, *Portrait Statuette of Mrs. Falk (Woman in Kimono)*, 1915-1916, bronze, The Tel Aviv Museum, The Erich Goeritz Collection.

moting the young industrialist's business interests. Falk served as a supplier for the German army command, buying up raw materials, particularly wool, and supplying material for uniforms.[10]

The painter George Grosz, who met Falk in 1917 through a mutual friend—German poet Theodore Däubler, a pioneer of expressionism in literature—remembers the young Falk, who became his patron,[11] as a decisive and dynamic person, intolerant of opposition. Grosz described him as an "oriental type" who loved art and the company of artists. At the same time, he was on friendly terms with generals and army officers, contacts that were surely helpful to him in furthering his business interests. He invested the money he earned from his dealings with the army in a large and valuable art collection.[12] It was Falk's desire to use his money to acquire "things of the spirit," unlike the "riffraff, glutted with profits, who only understand how to amass multi-figure sums," as he wrote to Gustav F. Hartlaub, the government appointee in charge of the Kunsthalle Mannheim at the time.[13]

Within the span of only two years, between 1915 and 1917, Falk managed to put together a collection that included works by impressionists (Renoir, Degas), post-impressionists (van Gogh, Cézanne, Gauguin, Signac) and other French artists (Rousseau, Redon, Picasso, Chagall, Derain), as well as expressionists (Munch, Marc, Feininger, Kandinsky, Kokoschka). To these he added a large number of works by the sculptor Wilhelm Lehmbruck, and paintings by George Grosz.

In an article on the Falk Collection published in the *Kunstblatt* in 1918, Paul Westheim lauds it for its orientation toward contemporary art, an example of a new generation of collectors. The collection is described as "a gallery pointing clearly and convincingly to the liveliest artistic activity of its times."[14] It is not depicted as a collection presuming to reflect any particular artistic development in a consistent manner, or as one guided by considerations of any artistic policy. Falk's approach to art and to his collection is portrayed as intimate, based on personal involvement, and highlighting the creative experience. He is described as being interested in a particular item, rather than the total output of the artist, attempting to acquire the best works of the artist he collected. Thus, for example, as Westheim mentions, Falk did not seek out just any van Gogh, but specifically *L'Arlésienne*. He tenaciously sought to acquire works exemplifying the essence of the artist's work. Westheim claims that the collection evolved by virtue of an artistic instinct, accompanied by admirable self-confidence. In amassing his collection, Falk disregarded the advice of art scholars, whether it came from his friend Däubler, from Westheim, or from Hartlaub.[15] His choice was intuitive, based on the immediate impression of a work rather than on any informed or rational approach.

At the Kunsthalle Mannheim, Falk was greatly appreciated as a collector. In a letter to Weichert, the director of the Kunsthalle (then in the army in The Hague), Hartlaub wrote in reference to the exhibition *From Private Collections in Mannheim:* "Even if it does not encourage collecting in grand style, the way Mr. Falk does, it does promote, at the very least, the purchase of art without prejudice and with good taste."[16]

Falk was friendly with Wilhelm Lehmbruck and his family, and served as patron to the sculptor. He first met Lehmbruck in 1915.[17] Falk provided the sculptor with a monthly allowance and, in return, selected several of his works for his collection every year.[18] Manfred Lehmbruck, the artist's son, vividly recalls the friendship that existed between his parents and the Falks,[19] the generous invitations proffered by the industrialist, and the extraordinary chic of Adèle Falk (fig. 12).[20] This childhood impression is confirmed by George Grosz' comparison of Mrs. Falk to a "rare bird of paradise."[21]

Fig. 12. Mrs. Falk (standing), Mrs. Lehmbruck (seated), and the three Lehmbruck children (from left to right: Gustav, Gido, and Manfred), 1917, Arosa.

103

Left: Fig. 13. Wilhelm Lehmbruck, *Seated Youth (The Friend)*, 1917, composite tinted plaster, National Gallery of Art, Washington, Andrew W. Mellon Fund.

Right: Fig. 14. Wilhelm Lehmbruck, *Kneeling Woman*, 1911, cast stone, The Museum of Modern Art, Abby Aldrich Rockefeller Fund.

Wilhelm Lehmbruck produced several portraits of Sally and Adèle Falk; at least two portraits in sculpture of Sally Falk and four of his wife, as well as numerous drawings and prints of them both, can be found in the Lehmbruck Museum and other collections.[22] *Portrait of Mr. F.*, 1915–1916, in bronze, and a terra-cotta statuette, called *Portrait Statuette of Mrs. Falk (Woman in Kimono)*, 1915–1916, were in Falk's possession and became part of the Goeritz Collection donated to the Tel Aviv Museum.[23] Lehmbruck scholar Dietrich Schubert considers the Falk sculptures among the major works of their kind in the artist's oeuvre. They "compress the form and seek to express the internal."[24]

In the winter of 1916, the Kunsthalle Mannheim mounted a large exhibition of Wilhelm Lehmbruck's work. Sally Falk took an active part in the preparations for the exhibition and anonymously lent thirty-three pieces to it. It was then that his contacts with Hartlaub and the Kunsthalle were established; this relationship became increasingly close. It was agreed that Falk would assist the Kunsthalle in expanding its collection of contemporary sculpture through the acquisition of German and international pieces, with the emphasis on German sculpture. Falk began by acquiring six of Lehmbruck's works, *Seated Youth (The Friend)*,

1917 (National Gallery of Art, Washington, fig. 13),[25] and *Kneeling Woman*, 1911 (Museum of Modern Art, New York, figs. 14–15),[26] among them.[27] He later added three works by Edwin Scharff, Georg Kolbe, and Ernesto di Fiori.[28]

The Falk donation formed the nucleus of the Kunsthalle Mannheim's modern sculpture collection, which was one of the major and most comprehensive collections of early twentieth-century German sculpture. In early 1917, an agreement was signed between the industrialist Sally Falk and the city of Mannheim, according to which the nine sculptures mentioned above would be on loan to the Kunsthalle and would become a gift no later than 21 January 1921. In 1921, the clause providing for the gift came into effect, and the sculpture became the property of the city of Mannheim.[29]

Sally Falk's success as a businessman was short-lived. Faced with financial difficulties, his company was liquidated in July 1917. At the beginning of 1918, he was forced to sell a large part of his art collection in order to pay his debts. Among the fifty paintings, over one hundred and fifty graphics and watercolors, and fifteen pieces of sculpture sold, were valuable paintings by van Gogh, Cézanne, El Greco, and Picasso. Although the Kunsthalle Mannheim expressed an interest in acquiring

Fig. 15. A room in the "Degenerate Art" exhibition, Munich, 1937, with Wilhelm Lehmbruck's *Kneeling Woman*

these items,[30] Falk turned the matter over to Paul Cassirer, a Berlin art dealer. The packing list of the shipment sent to Cassirer, today in the Kunsthalle archives, along with the reproductions in the *Kunstblatt*, make it possible to reconstruct that part of the collection which was transferred to him. It included, among other pieces, two works by Archipenko as well as oil paintings by Grosz, Chagall, Kandinsky, Klee, Boccioni, and Léger. In reference to this sale, Falk wrote to Hartlaub, ". . . we may be able to save several works of art. . . . They will serve as the basis for my new collection toward which I plan to work after I have recovered."[31] This was a declaration of intention on the part of Falk and one which he seems to have successfully acted on within a relatively short time in Geneva.

While seeking a solution to his financial problems, Falk was making preparations to leave Germany for Switzerland. Most likely in order to evade the tax authorities, to whom he owed 172,000 German marks[32] (a debt he never paid), and probably out of fear of mobilization into the army, Falk entered a sanatorium for lung diseases, in Arosa.[33] In February 1919, the customs and duties office of the state of Baden seized the property of Sally Falk.[34] The agreement he had signed with the city of Mannheim in 1917 protected his donation from confiscation by the tax authorities even though in 1919 it was still only a promised gift. Before the attachment order was issued, however, Falk had managed to transfer the remainder of his private collection to the ownership of a Swiss business contact, Rudolf Pfrunder. Pfrunder, described by Anita Lehmbruck, the artist's widow, as a man who knew nothing about art,[35] sold the entire collection *en masse* to the Berlin art dealer J. Ber Neumann for the sum of 60,000 German marks.[36] The packing list of the shipment to Pfrunder, prepared by the Kunsthalle, where the collection was temporarily stored, completes the reconstruction of the entire Falk Collection in its German period. The list includes one drawing by Archipenko. Several sculptures were not offered for sale by Pfrunder, apparently at Falk's request, perhaps because of their personal value. Among these were Lehmbruck's *Portrait of Mrs. Falk*, in marble, *Portrait of Mr. F.*, in bronze, and *Portrait Statuette of Mrs. Falk (Woman in Kimono)*, a terra-cotta statuette.[37] These seem to have been sent to Falk. The last two are today in the Tel Aviv Museum collection.

In 1919, Sally Falk settled in Geneva and set up a new textile firm, S.G. Falk.[38] Manfred Lehmbruck related that after the death of his father in 1919, the warm relations between his mother and the Falks abruptly ended.[39] It was his belief that Falk refrained from conducting any correspondence with Germany so as not to reveal his whereabouts.[40]

Aside from the works today in the Tel Aviv Museum collection, we have no information about art collections that may have been acquired by Falk during his Swiss period. It may be assumed that Falk acquired most of the Archipenko works while in Geneva, although it is possible that some were forwarded from Germany. It would seem that, as a result of the debts he left behind in Germany, Falk was forced to begin a new career both as a businessman and as a collector in Geneva under a new name—George Falk. The dynamism and unerring instincts that had served him so well in amassing his collections in Mannheim once again proved themselves in Geneva. Thus, in the 1920s, he became the major collector of the works of Alexander Archipenko.

Archipenko was working in France between 1908 and 1921, yet his work was not enthusiastically received by French collectors. In his European years (until 1923), Archipenko's work was in demand mostly by German collectors. Although he participated in important group exhibitions in France, the appreciation he earned there came almost exclusively from several of his fellow artists and a small circle of writers and art critics, among them Blaise Cendrars, Maurice Raynal, and Iwan Goll. Most of the work he managed to sell at this time was bought by artists and writers who he was acquainted with or was on close terms with, including Guillaume Apollinaire, Marie Laurencin, Fernand Léger, and Alberto Magnelli.

Archipenko's first patron in Germany was Karl-Ernst Osthaus. Osthaus held Archipenko's first large show (together with Le Fauconnier) in the Folkwang Museum in Hagen in 1912/1913, at which time he also purchased two of his sculptures. The artist's second patron was Herwarth Walden, who mounted the second major Archipenko exhibition, *Alexandre Archipenko, Siebzehnte Ausstellung*, in Der Sturm Gallery, Berlin in September 1913. He purchased four of the artist's sculptures and several drawings.[41] In this and another exhibition held in Der Sturm Gallery in 1921, Walden exhibited the plaster relief, *Sketch for Ceiling*, 1913 (cat. no. 12). Eva Spector, of Tel Aviv, who was the gallery's secretary from 1922 to 1929, bought the relief in 1925.[42] She later sold it to Sam and Ayala Zacks, and in 1983 it was presented as a gift to the Tel Aviv Museum by Mrs. Zacks-Abramov and was thus added to the collection.

Falk's interest in sculpture prompted him, while still in Mannheim, to acquire works by Alexander Archipenko. It appears to have been Lehmbruck, who became friendly with Archipenko in Paris in 1910, who later introduced him to Falk.[43] If so, initial contact between the two must have taken place between 1915 and 1919, the year Lehmbruck died. Falk's collection in Mannheim included two of Archipenko's sculptural works and at least one drawing.[44]

It was only after 1920, in Geneva, that the few random acquisitions became the basis for a full-scale collection. Eventually, over the course of a few years, Falk would become the owner of scores of Archipenko's early works,[45] most of them of exceptional quality.

From November to December 1919, Archipenko held a one-man show in the Librairie Kundig in Geneva; the exhibition later traveled to the Zurich Kunsthaus. We can reasonably assume that Falk saw the exhibition and may have already owned at least four of the works in it, since they are listed in the catalogue as belonging to a private Swiss collection.[46] On this occasion, it is likely that Falk met with Archipenko, who was in Switzerland for the exhibition. Archipenko returned to Geneva in late 1920, when he participated in the "International Exhibition of Modern Art," held at the Bâtiment électoral.[47] From Geneva, he wrote to Marcel Duchamp in New York regarding his exhibition planned by the Société Anonyme for 1921. In this letter, dated 16 January 1921, Archipenko informed Duchamp that he had sold the large sculpto-painting he sent Duchamp for reproduction—*Woman*—and several other works.[48] (*Woman*, cat. no. 31, appeared on the back cover of the catalogue of the Archipenko exhibition organized by the Société Anonyme in New York in 1921.) In addition to the pieces he bought at the Librairie Kundig, Falk apparently purchased about seven other works at the second exhibition in Geneva.[49]

On one of these visits to Geneva, Archipenko created the painted plaster sculpture, *Double Portrait/Mr. and Mrs. Falk*, as well as the *Portrait of Mrs. Falk* in wax, which bears the dedication from Archipenko "to Mme. Falk, 1920, Geneva." It is reasonable to assume that, at this time, the Falks already owned a large collection of Archipenko's work (it seems, even then, that they owned more than any other collector), which would explain the artist's gratitude and his dedication of the portrait to Mrs. Falk. From the catalogues of other early exhibitions, it is evident that Falk also acquired other works in the early 1920s.[50]

During the second half of the 1920s, Falk was again plagued by financial difficulties, and he was compelled to sell or transfer part of his collection to his creditors, the works of Archipenko, a construction by Henri Laurens, and several Lehmbruck sculptures among them. Apparently at this time, he was forced to leave Switzerland and move to France. His finances did not improve, and he had no choice but to periodically sell the works of art he still possessed. Thus, in 1960 Falk sold three watercolors by George Grosz to the Kunsthalle Mannheim.[51]

It was probably due to the French citizenship of his Marseilles-born wife that Sally Falk, the native German, was allowed to spend the years during World War II in France. Schiller notes that it was only there, as clarified by the Mannheim city archives, that Falk was safe from the Gestapo.[52] For a while after the war he lived in Monte Carlo, and later, in San Remo. The state of his health, as well as his finances, was very poor. The city of Mannheim, later recognized his important contribution to the Kunsthalle collections in 1917 and awarded him an honorarium which was paid to him beginning 1 April 1961.[53] Sally Falk died in San Remo in 1962. His widow, Adèle, returned to Marseilles, where she continued to receive the monthly payments from Germany until her death in 1972.[54] The Falks were childless.

If Sally Falk displayed daring and intuition in the choice of artists represented in his collection, and sensitivity and unerring instinct in selecting their works, it was the generosity, caution, intelligence, and historical foresight of Erich Goeritz, along with his deep interest in both art and Zionism, that enabled this important and rare collection to survive.

We do not know today whether there was any direct contact between Goeritz and Falk through their business association; however, in the late 1920s, Goeritz came to own a collection of more than thirty art works (most of them by Archipenko) which had once belonged to Falk. Andrew Goeritz recalls his mother telling him that his father received the collection by way of payment of a debt, but he is very doubtful as to whether it came directly from Falk himself.[55]

In 1933, with the rise of Hitler to power in Germany, Goeritz sent a large portion of his collection to Tel Aviv, both in order to save it from the danger that threatened it in Europe and to come to the aid of the young museum, founded only one year earlier. Goeritz was therefore one of the first collectors to respond to the appeal of Karl Schwarz, the first director of the Tel Aviv Museum, who called on collectors in Europe to contribute to the development of the new museum. In this manner, the collection was saved and did not share the fate of many other collections of modern art, which remained in Germany only to be destroyed, confiscated, or lost.

Erich Goeritz,[56] a contemporary of Sally Falk, was born in Chemnitz in Saxony, Germany in 1889, and was the eldest son of the textile manufacturer, Sigmund Goeritz. As a youth he displayed a general interest in art—drawing, painting, music, and literature. At an early age he was already involved in Zionist activities in Chemnitz. After a period of apprenticeship in Breslau, he joined his father's textile firm and later became its manager. During World War I, the Goeritz textile factory supplied undergarments to the German army. The firm continued to prosper after the war and became one of the leaders of the German textile industry. In 1918, Erich Goeritz married Senta Sternberger, and that same year, their first child, Thomas, was born. Their second son,

Andrew, was born two years later. In 1920, the family moved from Munich to Berlin. Their home in Berlin soon became a meeting place for artists, collectors, and art lovers. Several of the artists in their circle portrayed Senta and Erich Goeritz. Lovis Corinth produced a number of paintings, drawings, and etchings of Goeritz with his wife (fig. 16) and with his friend, the collector David Leder. The sculptor Edwin Scharff also produced a portrait of the couple. Max Liebermann painted Senta Goeritz several times. The Tel Aviv Museum collection includes *Portrait of Erich Goeritz* in bronze by Edwin Scharff, two portraits in oil of Mrs. Goeritz (1928 and 1931) by Max Liebermann, a charcoal drawing of Erich Goeritz by Lovis Corinth, and two color lithographs, one of Erich Goertiz and the other of his wife, also by Lovis Corinth. The Goeritz textile mill in Chemnitz is the subject of a large oil painting in the museum collection, produced in 1927 by Jakob Steinhardt.

Influenced by his friend Max Liebermann, Goeritz bought several impressionist paintings; in 1924 he purchased Manet's *Bar at the Folies-Bergère* (which was later sold to Samuel Courtauld and donated to the Courtauld Institute Galleries in London). Goeritz' collection also included works by Degas, Toulouse-Lautrec, Monet, Pissarro, and Cézanne. Among the German artists in his collection were Ernst Barlach, Lovis Corinth, Georg Ehrlich, Konrad Felixmüller, Erich Heckel, Oskar Kokoschka, Wilhelm Lehmbruck, Max Liebermann, Ludwig Meidner, Edwin Scharff, Karl Schmidt-Rottluff, and Jakob Steinhardt. To these he added, in the late 1920s, about thirty works by Archipenko that had once belonged to Falk.

In 1933 Goeritz, determined to leave Germany, first sent his wife and sons to France, preparing to join them later. He shipped most of his art collection (except for about a dozen pieces) to the Tel Aviv Museum in response to the appeal of Karl Schwarz, who, prior to his arrival in Tel Aviv in 1933, was director of the Jewish Museum in Berlin and was acquainted with Goeritz and his collection. In August 1933, Goeritz wrote to Schwarz: "I have become somewhat skeptical, whether it is not already too late."[57] But the works of art were sent off in September, and on 16 November 1933, Schwarz informed Goeritz in Berlin that they had been enthusiastically received in Tel Aviv. He also mentioned a cable signed by the mayor of Tel Aviv, Meir Dizengoff, acknowledging receipt of the collection. Goeritz left Germany in 1934, leaving behind property that was subsequently confiscated by the Nazis. He transferred his business interests to Luxembourg and France, and then to England, where he settled with his family in London in 1939. With the help of his two sons, he reestablished his textile firm in England.

Fig. 16. Lovis Corinth, *Portrait of Mr. and Mrs. Erich Goeritz*, 1922, oil on canvas, Insel Hombroich Collection.

The Goeritz Collection, originally on loan to the museum for two years, remained in Tel Aviv for more than twenty years. In 1955 Goeritz was to visit Tel Aviv to discuss the future of his collection,[58] but he died shortly after informing the museum of his proposed visit. Following his death in April 1955, his family donated a large part of the collection to the museum in his memory—some five hundred items including sculpture and paintings by Archipenko, Degas, Lehmbruck, Barlach, Laurens, Liebermann, Kokoschka, and Steinhardt, and prints by several German expressionists, among them Schmidt-Rottluff, Ludwig Meidner, Erich Heckel, and Lovis Corinth.

The Sculpture and Sculpto-Paintings of Alexander Archipenko from the Tel Aviv Museum Collection

ARCHIPENKO'S WORKS IN THE Goeritz Collection are unique not only for their quality, rarity, and concentration in one location, but also because they systematically demonstrate the development of Archipenko's early work in France between 1910 and 1921. The collection also illustrates the diverse media in which Archipenko worked in Europe, ranging from sculpture in plaster, terra-cotta, and bronze to sculpto-paintings and polychromed modeled sculpture, as well as preparatory drawings and oil paintings. The works chosen for the present exhibition can be considered milestones in the development of Archipenko's style and his unique contribution to modern sculpture.

The subject of all of the works in the collection is the human form, particularly the female figure. Despite the extreme abstraction toward which Archipenko gradually moved, he consistently preserved the characteristic features of the human image, albeit in the most symbolic manner.

The earliest work by Alexander Archipenko in the Tel Aviv Museum collection is *Kneeling Woman*, 1910 (cat. no. 2). Made of bronze, *Kneeling Woman* is refined in its elegant, elongated form; it is freed from the block. The delicate curves of the female figure are a departure from the compact blocklike archaic forms typical of Archipenko's early carved figures (such as *Sorrow*, 1909, cat. no. 1, and *Mother and Child*, 1910–1911, cat. no. 3). However, the sculpture still contains one element reminiscent of the early group: the treatment of the head, tightly encircled by the arm framing it. Werner Hofmann wrote of the evolution of this motif and of its historical sources:

. . . Anatomically viewed, the human skull diminishes and weakens the compact bulk of the torso; it is an appendage, which seems, like the arms and legs, to be striving to get away from the core of the body, and in which the universal is transformed into the particular—a physiognomy. From the beginning, the Cubists were concerned with finding a common denominator for all the limbs. In attempting to reunite the head with the torso, they went back to an ancient motif most strikingly represented by the *Dying Niobe* in the Terme Museum, Rome: the arm, with the elbow crooked sharply above the head, not only encloses the head but, beyond this, shapes the body into a wedge. Michelangelo took up the motif in *The Dying Slave*, in the Louvre. A work formerly ascribed to him, the so-called *Ecorché*, transmitted this motif to Cézanne and perhaps also to Gauguin. Soon thereafter it appeared in early Cubism in the works of Picasso, Archipenko and Gaudier-Brzeska.[59]

The pose of *Kneeling Woman*, with its arm folded like a wedge

Fig. 17. Greek, *Dying Niobid*, c. 450-440 B.C., Museo Nazionale Romano, Rome.

around the head, as well as the stance of the legs—each are at a right angle, at varying heights, in a posture somewhere between kneeling and rising—clearly brings to mind the classic *Dying Niobid* (fig. 17). Yet, while the classical sculpture expresses movement and emotion (the dying Niobid struggles to remove the arrow from her back and shows pathos on her face), Archipenko's treatment of the human body stresses the formal design, clarity of the composition, and mass-space relationships. The upper part of the figure, the raised arm and the head, are serenely static, while a certain potential movement is apparent in the somewhat exaggerated, hipshot position and the implied rising motion of the legs and feet.

Although the female nude is a common theme in neoclassical and impressionist sculpture, Archipenko has departed from the academic or impressionist treatment of the subject. The figurative element still predominates and the human body is still whole, but the forms are clearly stylized and the composition geometric, constructed of a series of triangles balancing each other. The anatomical details are similarly geometric—conical breasts, triangular stomach, and schematically squared off hands and feet. The masses are simplified and reduced to the essentials.

This bronze version of *Kneeling Woman* is the only cast of the work known today. Katherine Michaelsen notes that, according to the catalogues of Archipenko's early exhibitions, with only one exception (*Vintagers*, 1909), the artist never showed any bronze sculpture before 1920, having worked mainly in plaster and terra-cotta, and occasionally in cement, marble, or wood. It seems that it was not until 1920 that Archipenko cast a number of his works in bronze (several bronzes appeared that year for the first time in the Venice Biennale). It was probably due to economic considerations that he did not cast his sculptures in bronze before this time.[60] Thus, *Kneeling Woman* could have been cast in bronze only in 1920, ten years after it had first been created. The work exhibited in the 1919–1920 show in Geneva and Zurich is described as a plaster in the catalogue, whereas in the catalogues of the Der Sturm exhibition of 1921 and an exhibition in Frankfurt in 1922, it is listed as a bronze.

The "partial figure" in modern sculpture was treated in depth in the writings of Albert Elsen.[61] Along with Brancusi, Archipenko was one of the first twentieth-century sculptors to create figures originally conceived of as "partial," rather than as ones whose limbs or head were eliminated in a process of editing the work, as Rodin was wont to do. "For Archipenko, the missing limb won him a new continuity of ara-

113

besque and elegance and a space consciousness on the part of the viewer, who instinctively looked for the entire figure."[62]

Archipenko's conception of the partial figure is evident in his oil painting *The Dance*, 1912–1913 (fig. 18), in the Tel Aviv Museum. This painting is clearly a study for sculpture and is related to a series of sculptures on the same subject, most specifically *Red Dance*, 1912–1913 (illustrated p. 22, fig. 2). From this preparatory painting it is clear that even in the initial stage, the artist conceived of the subject as a partial figure.

The earliest example of a partial figure in the Tel Aviv Museum collection is *Bather (Seated Woman)*, 1912 (cat. no. 4). The arms of this terra-cotta female figure—here in a stance somewhere between sitting and kneeling—are missing above the elbow, and the legs are cut off at the ankle. Clearly, *Bather* was originally conceived as a partial figure; the broad thighs and high waist create a heavy triangular mass that is highly expressive precisely because of the lack of hands and feet, which, if included, would have detracted from the central mass. Serving no function in the movement depicted, they are thus unnecessary. The partial left arm, longer than the right, throws the weight of the figure to

114

Fig. 19. Paul Cézanne, *Bathers*, c. 1890, oil on canvas, Musée d'Orsay, Paris.

the left and forward, thus emphasizing the leftward and downward direction of the motion and force.

Bather not only illustrates Archipenko's use of the partial figure but also displays his novel and interesting approach to the base. No longer is the base merely a neutral square, external to the sculpture; rather, it is an integral part of the work. The female figure appears to be sliding off the base. She is seated or kneeling upon it in a contrapposto stance with her legs extended downward and outward. The figure interacts with the base: the legs are pressed together, gripping the base, while the upper part of the body—the torso, shoulders, and head—twist sharply in the opposite direction. The base becomes a springboard for a spiral movement of the entire body, which seems to be surging upward.[63]

As the prototype for the figure and composition of *Bather*, Archipenko may have used one of the figures in Cézanne's painting, *The Bathers*, c. 1890 (fig. 19), now in the Louvre, which he could have seen in Ambroise Vollard's gallery in Paris.[64]

The mass of *Bather* is defined by its spatial qualities. The geometric head—an abstract sphere—represents a more advanced, abstract stage in the simplification of form than is found in *Kneeling Woman*, 1910. The features are implied by two recessed arcs, hinting at eyebrows and nose. One's attention is caught by the reduced proportions of the round head in relation to the rest of the body, and by the repetition of the form in the rounded right knee.[65]

In addition to the early terra-cotta version of *Bather* in Tel Aviv, there

115

is also an early plaster cast in the Karl-Ernst Osthaus Museum in Hagen, Germany. It was included in Archipenko's exhibition held in the Folkwang Museum in Hagen, as early as 1912/1913.

The third sculpture among the early works in the collection is the plaster *Repose*, 1912 (cat. no. 5), a compact female figure reclining in an odalisque position. The arm encircling the head, forming a wedge, and the reclining position of the body may have been inspired by a Hellenistic model, as it appears in the *Barberini Faun* (Glyptothek, Munich) or *Sleeping Ariadne* (Musée du Louvre, Paris, fig. 20).[66]

Roland Schacht was the first art historian to suggest a connection between *Repose* and Michelangelo's reclining figure of *Dawn* on the tomb of Lorenzo de' Medici.[67] Although the arms are in different positions, several elements are quite similar: the poses of the female figures reclining on their backs in precarious equilibrium; the twist of the shoulders; and the muscular midsections of the body.[68]

The composition of *Repose* is more compact than that of *Kneeling Woman* or *Bather*, but in contrast to Archipenko's earlier works—which are archaic, blocklike, and closed—its contours are rounded, flowing, and refined, and the body as a whole languidly unfolds and opens outward. *Repose* is a frontal sculpture, yet the back is molded and even contains a linear incision depicting, in fragmented and elusive line, a lovemaking couple.[69]

The interrelationship between this sculpture and its base is of particular interest. The figure seems to be sinking into the "soft," almost sensual support-background which constitutes both its base and an integral part of the sculpture itself. Its undulating forms merge with the base in

116

which the same soft contours are repeated. As with the figure, the base —and the figure's integration with it—may have been inspired by a Hellenistic model, such as that in *Sleeping Ariadne*. This interrelationship marks an evolution toward "the passing of the pedestal: bringing sculpture down to earth," as Albert Elsen defines it.[70]

A second plaster cast of *Repose* was apparently made from the same mold as this cast. The work also exists in terra-cotta (dated 1911 by the artist) in Frances Archipenko Gray's collection. A marble version, originally in the Folkwang Museum in Hagen (the collection was later moved to Essen), was confiscated by the Nazis, and its present location is unknown. These various versions were shown alternately in early exhibitions. The plaster version in the Tel Aviv Museum was tinted light pink by the artist in order to make it appear more like terra-cotta. Donald Karshan suggests that it may have been this copy that the artist sent to the historic Armory Show in New York in 1913, as it is known that the sculpture exhibited there appeared to be a light-colored terra-cotta. (According to installation photographs of the Armory Show, *Repose* stood on a table beside Brancusi's *Madame Pogany* and Archipenko's statuette *Negress*.)[71]

The three early works we have considered thus far display Archipenko's simplification of form but do not yet reflect the influence of cubism. In the next group of modeled sculptures, this influence is already discernible in the simultaneous points of view, the faceting of the surfaces, the substitution of void for mass through the interchange of convex and concave forms, and the opening up of the monolithic block.

The relief *Sketch for Ceiling* is the earliest work in this cubist-inspired group in the collection. It is a high relief in plaster with a dense and complex composition in which four female nudes are intertwined on several spatial planes. The figure in the foremost plane bisects the square composition diagonally from corner to corner. The other three figures, beneath or behind her, appear interwoven at right angles to each other on nonparallel planes. They seem to be floating, perhaps falling. The anatomical structure is reduced to rounded geometric forms— cones and cylinders—lacking any detail, while the background is constructed of sharp crystalline forms with triangular facets. The artist's use of solid geometric shapes in high relief in white plaster creates dramatic effects of light and shadow, which become a predominant element. None of the figures in the composition is complete; their limbs or heads are alternately cut off or missing in a range of variations. Where the neck and head are not cut off, as is the case with two of the figures, a sin-

117

gle elliptical unit is formed without the slightest hint of features, not even shadows. In the headless figures, the partial arm approximates the shape of the head, forming something that might be a bent head, shoulder, or breast. The omission of some of the extremities adds to the harmony of the composition, enhancing its cohesiveness by the ambiguity and interpenetration of its separate components. The figures are intertwined in a very powerful and dynamic composition—almost futurist in its simultaneity—in which the separation between one figure and the next or between a figure and the background is not always clear.

This interpenetration of forms, in which solid and void are equivalent, is one aspect often found in cubist sculpture. Another feature common in cubist sculpture and painting is the simultaneous depiction of the object from various vantage points. Thus, for instance, the central diagonal figure is presented here from three or four different angles: the upper part of the body is seen from the front, in a three-quarter view, with one breast pointing upward, while the legs are presented from behind, showing the folds at the back of the knees and the rear muscles of the leg; the foot is seen from below as a concave arch, and the ankle is seen in profile.

Sketch for Ceiling is the only extant example of an architectural project in which Archipenko was involved.[72] The motivation to create an architectural relief may have come from Archipenko's association with the Puteaux group, with whom he met on Sundays in Puteaux as early as 1911.[73] The concepts of the unity of the arts and the relationship between art and real life were important to these artists, who displayed an interest in architectural design and decoration.[74] Duchamp-Villon created a series of architectural reliefs between 1911 and 1913, the most famous of which is *The Lovers*, 1913 (fig. 21). It is a low relief made with a cubist vocabulary of forms, including fragmentation and faceting. In 1912 he designed the façade for a private home which came to be known as the *Maison Cubiste*, and he exhibited the model for it in the Salon d'Automne of 1912. Several of the members of the Puteaux group, led by André Maré, designed and exhibited the interior of the house.[75] Duchamp-Villon's relief *The Lovers* was shown in the Salon d'Automne in Paris in 1913, the year it was produced. Both reliefs—*The Lovers* and *Sketch for Ceiling*—share several features in addition to the date of their creation, including dismembered figures, geometric representation of anatomical features which are reduced and abstracted, and a composition based on internal movement and space-mass relationships. Archipenko's composition, however, is more complex, tight, and dynamic than is Duchamp-Villon's and consists of several spatial planes.

Sketch for Ceiling was exhibited in Archipenko's one-man show at

Der Sturm Gallery in Berlin, in September 1913 (no. 21 in the catalogue). A price list in the catalogue notes: in plaster—M 500, in bronze —M 650, and in marble—M 650.[76] This information leads one to believe that there was more than one version of the work. Mrs. Eva Spector remembers seeing several versions in the gallery.[77]

Sketch for Ceiling is the earliest relief created by Archipenko. Shortly after he had completed it, the artist began to work intensively on reliefs, in a series of works he called sculpto-paintings, most of which he produced by the technique of assemblage but others in painted plaster or papier-mâché.

Leaning Woman (Penché) (cat. no. 13), a chromium-plated bronze sculpture, also belongs to the cubist-inspired modeled sculpture group. In the past it was dated 1911 in the Tel Aviv Museum; this is in agreement with Archipenko's own dating in his book, *Fifty Creative Years*.[78] Due to new considerations, however, the date has been revised to 1913–1914. This revision was based on the dating of the piece in the catalogue of the Der Sturm exhibition in Berlin in 1921, as well as on stylistic considerations.[79]

This sculpture represents a female figure reduced to an arched series of conical and tubular forms. The figure, firmly anchored to its base, leans dynamically out into space. The head is oval and lacks specific features; the body is tubular and armless. The surface is streamlined, polished to a bright, smooth finish. The anatomical details and female characteristics are reduced in order to highlight the leaning movement, introduced here as the most prominent feature of the composition for

119

the first time in Archipenko's work.

This sculpture represents an interesting phase in the artist's experimentation with space-mass relationships. By bending its slim schematic silhouette into a quarter-circle, marking and outlining space, Archipenko conceived his figure as a frame for space. Thus, the space itself becomes a positive value. (At a later stage, Archipenko would do precisely the opposite: parts of the human body would be outlined from without by mass and themselves become a void, such as in *Statuette*, 1915 [cat. no. 19].)

The arc, precariously rising over and beyond the base, creates tension and a certain degree of unease in the mind of the viewer because the center of gravity of the sculpture appears to be remote from the base. In fact, the base is wider at the bottom and a triangular bracket provides an additional support, thus stabilizing the sculpture.

The arched silhouette of *Leaning Woman* appeared earlier in sculptures by Archipenko that have not survived—*Salome*, 1910 (fig. 22),

120

and *Red Dance.* Here, however, the leaning movement is bolder, the contours are more abstract and reduced, and the arms are totally omitted. The three works reveal a gradual progression from a relatively naturalistic representation in *Salome,* in which the anatomical details are still apparent (though the limbs are truncated), through *Red Dance,* in which the anatomical structure is stretched, elongated, reduced, and more geometric, to the extremely geometric and abstract *Leaning Woman.*

The chromium-plated bronze version in the Tel Aviv Museum is one of two bronze versions of the sculpture that are documented in the early literature. In addition, a gilt plaster version is known to have existed but is now lost.

Statue on Triangular Base (Statuette), 1914 (cat. no. 15), can be considered a rare, single copy; there is no record of another early version of this work. It is an important example of the cubist syntax Archipenko employed during this period. The figure stands on a pyramidal base echoed in the form comprising the head, neck, and shoulder unit, which is shaped like a funnel or cone pointed sharply at the top. A wedge-shaped section has been cut from this cone to indicate the separation of head from shoulder. A half-sphere, representing a single breast, is attached on the left to the cone representing the head-neck-shoulder unit. This spherical form, shown somewhat flatter, recurs in the composition as the left knee. The figure is constructed of flat, geometric and sharply-edged facets and of overlapping convex and concave surfaces, as in a low relief.

The surface of the sculpture is worked in a relieflike manner. Thus, for example, the single arm appears as a flat, square projection with three lines incised in the hand to indicate fingers, while the kneecap resembles a flat disk superimposed onto the leg. Archipenko was already working in the construction technique he used for his sculpto-paintings when he created this work. Although *Statue on Triangular Base* was modeled in plaster, it gives the impression of having been assembled from separate parts pasted together, as in the sculpto-paintings.

Due to the surface projections and shallow depressions, the effect of light and shadow is a vital element in the perception of this work. In this emphasis on optical, rather than tactile qualities there is a similarity to the sculpto-paintings of this period, which we shall consider below.

Although the figure is fragmented and faceted, it remains faithful to the natural anatomical divisions, rhythms, and proportions of the body. The contrapposto stance of the figure adds delicacy, balance, and elegance to the composition.

121

The sculpture itself is freestanding and in-the-round, an effect em-
phasized by the triangular base on which the figure appears to pivot on
its axis. Rather than serving as a neutral element, distinct from the figure, the triangular base of the sculpture seems to continue the rhythm of
the body; the sculpture appears to be growing out of its base.

Statuette, 1915 (cat. no. 19), in terra-cotta, is the earliest example of a
polychromed sculpture in the Goeritz Collection. It was preceded by
Carrousel Pierrot, 1913 (polychromed plaster, illustrated p. 26, fig. 6).
As with other examples from this period, the artist was not content with
the natural color of the material and painted it various shades in an attempt to enhance the quality and cohesiveness of the sculpture. Thus,
for example, Archipenko made the head appear smaller and denser by
painting its upper portion and part of the sides of the frame surrounding
it in a darker tone. Later, he would continue painting his sculptures in
polychrome for purposes of design, as well as for illusionistic ends.

The most significant innovation in *Statuette,* however, as compared
to the preceding works in the collection, is the substitution of void for
mass. Archipenko removed material from the mass, going so far as to
create a hole—an elliptical void surrounded by mass—which represents
a positive form. In this manner, the void becomes synonymous with
mass. Archipenko wrote:

Traditionally there was a belief that sculpture begins where material touches
space. Thus space was understood as a kind of frame around the mass . . . .
Ignoring this tradition, I experimented, using the reverse idea and concluded
that sculpture may begin where space is encircled by the material . . . .[80]

The artist employed interchanging convex and concave surfaces, using
negative space in place of mass. The woman's chest is scooped out in a
rounded recess in which, by contrast, the convex single breast stands
out. In addition, one leg is represented by a massive cylinder jutting out
from the torso, while the other is represented by a depression. Thus, one
form becomes the negative of the other.

Between 1914 and 1917, Archipenko conducted highly original experiments investigating the various possibilities and the visual ambiguity of pairing and interchanging convex and concave surfaces. With
Statuette the artist made use of a concave form yet hints, by virtue of its
anatomical position, at a convex surface. It is precisely the form that is
missing that strengthens our awareness of the characteristic convexities
of the female anatomy.

The female figure, Archipenko's favorite theme, is the subject of all the works discussed so far. *Walking Soldier*, 1917 (cat. no. 27), is the only male figure in the Goeritz Collection. It was preceded by two earlier male figures, *Carrousel Pierrot*, 1913, and *Gondolier*, 1914 (illustrated p. 27, fig. 8), both of which show certain similarities with *Walking Soldier* in their sculptural conception.[81] All three are made of painted plaster and appear solid and monumental. In contrast to the convex and concave elements representing the sensual curves of the female body, the forms that predominate in the male figures are more rigid, mechanical, conical, and tubular. In *Walking Soldier* the mechanical forms are accompanied by an implied spiral, springlike motion, in contrast to the organic rhythm of the human body. The striding soldier is clothed in a military tunic, the tubular diagonal struts serving as his legs. The angle of the forward extended leg is continued in a narrow depression leading from the knee to the shoulder. As in *Gondolier*, where the oar and the leg are represented by a single unit, in *Walking Soldier* the legs are tubes which may also symbolize—in a manner less obvious than in *Gondolier*—weaponry or ammunition. The sense of a forward-flowing motion is heightened by the diagonal axis of the composition.

Archipenko's interpretation of the male figure is abstract and constitutes a departure from actual anatomy and the conventions of its representation. *Walking Soldier* is highly imaginative and charged with meaning beyond the formal aspect.

Produced during the war, *Walking Soldier* is Archipenko's only comment on this subject (the artist himself was remote from the events of the war, living between 1914 and 1918 in Nice). Michaelsen perceives the central element of the soldier's body as reminiscent of a rifle and interprets it as a visual metaphor for the soldier's dependence on his weapon.[82] Yet, despite its symbolism, formal considerations and space-mass relationships remain the central elements in this work.

Walking Soldier in the Tel Aviv Museum is the only early version of this sculpture (painted plaster, 40 centimeters high). Later, while in America, Archipenko cast a bronze edition, increasing its height to 1.17 meters. The plaster version, despite its smaller size, still appears monumental.

The polychromed plaster sculpture *Double Portrait / Mr. and Mrs. Falk*, 1920 (cat. no. 30), presents the Falks in profile, with Mrs. Falk in the foreground and her husband above and behind her. Sally (George) Falk, then thirty-two years old, and his wife Adèle are represented in an immediate way and in a manner closely resembling them in actuality.[83] George Grosz described Falk as a decisive and dynamic person who was domineering in his relations with his wife.[84] It is indeed as such that he appears in the portrait. In front of the Falks is a still life on a triangular tabletop; to the rear is a three-dimensional, sharply-angled architectural background which also functions as a frame for the figures. Although this is a modeled sculpture, most of the details are conveyed through the illusory medium of painting. The double portrait is a freestanding sculpture, but, because the back is unworked, it is best viewed from three sides only.

Two years later, Archipenko used the same medium—polychromed plaster—to create the portrait of his wife, Angelica (*Portrait of Artist's Wife*, 1922, illustrated p. 54, fig. 28). Again, he included in the composition a still life on a triangular tabletop in front of the figure and a similar architectural background behind it.

As noted before, the Tel Aviv Museum Collection also includes a wax statue representing the full figure of Mrs. Falk (fig. 9). It was dedicated by the artist to Mrs. Falk in Geneva in 1920, the same year in which it was created, during one of his visits to the city.[85] Apparently, at this time, the Falk Collection already contained a large number of the artist's works, and personal ties between the artist and the collector prevailed.

The sculptor Wilhelm Lehmbruck produced a large number of portraits of Sally and Adèle Falk in a more realistic style than that of the two Archipenko portraits. Of the two versions by Archipenko, the wax figure appears more realistic, although one arm is missing and the other, except for the hand, is represented by a concave form. The fact that Falk accepted these innovative and daring portraits is an indication of his open-mindedness as a patron.[86]

Seated Woman (Geometric Figure Seated), 1920 (cat. no. 29), is the last major modeled work produced in France by Archipenko before he moved to Berlin in 1921 (along with *Standing Woman* of the same year, whose present location is unknown). This work, which is modeled in plaster and painted in monochrome, represents the final, summarizing stage in a series of freestanding female figures Archipenko created under the influence of cubism and contains most of the characteristic features of his style in his late French period.

Although the figure in *Seated Woman* is still recognizable as a woman, in his interpretation of the female form Archipenko allowed himself free rein. Among the geometric forms in the composition, one can identify the head, the curves of the hips, a leg, a breast, and perhaps the arms, each part appearing in the vicinity of its true anatomical location. Nevertheless, the organic nature of the human form, its natural proportions, and inherent beauty, are no longer apparent. *Seated Woman* is a juxtaposition of tubular and mechanical masses—

convex and concave forms—and voids. Michaelsen notes that the mechanical quality of the figure is in accord with the spirit of its time and should particularly be seen in connection with Léger's postwar work, where the rounded volumes, recalling machine parts, are modeled in an illusionistic imitation of steel.[87]

Virtually each of the parts of the body appears more than once in the composition, first as mass, then as void. The head, for example, appears as both a massive rounded crown and as a rectangular hole. The body is shaped like a cello in both solid and void.

This sculpture is a conglomeration of the cubist-inspired forms Archipenko employed and developed beginning in 1913: well-defined, sharp angles and geometric surfaces; convex and concave forms interchanged, with the depressions more pronounced than before; and voids used as substitutes for mass in the composition. A dynamic equilibrium is achieved here in a complex architectonic structure in which the modeled mass appears constructed, as in assemblage. The work is freestanding and should be viewed from all sides, with each vantage point affording unexpected surprises.

Seated Woman clearly reflects the metaphysical quality Archipenko sought to express in his work; through the duality between mass and void, he succeeded in presenting that which physically exists as that which does not, and to give real form to that which seems not to exist—the void—in a manner which makes it equal in value to the mass.[88]

Archipenko painted the plaster dark red in order to highlight its sculpted quality. While he may also have chosen painted plaster because of economic considerations (as had been the case in the earlier period, when the price of the materials was an important consideration), with *Seated Woman* the color is more likely related to that of the polychromed sculpture in which the choice was purely aesthetic.

The final group of works to be considered, consisting of five sculpto-paintings, is characterized by the incorporation of painting and sculpture and the juxtaposition of concrete three-dimensional objects—including actual light and shadow—with the illusionistic painted image. These works were produced by the process of assemblage as part of a bold new conception of the sculpted mass, which involved its representation by more schematic means.

Woman with Fan, 1914 (cat. no. 17), is the earliest of Archipenko's surviving sculpto-paintings.[89] Affixed to its rear supporting panel, covered with burlap and oilcloth, are planks of wood, wooden poles and cones, bent sheet metal and ready-made objects—a metal funnel and a

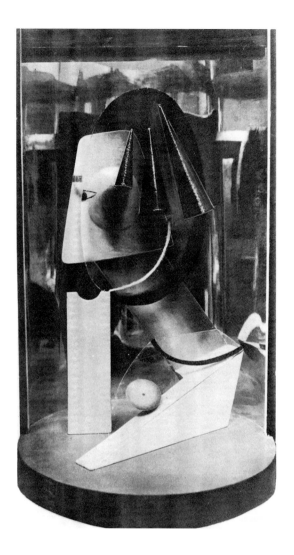

glass bottle—all painted in a range of bold colors.

Several of the ideas and inventive devices employed in this sculpto-painting also appear in Archipenko's early constructions: *Portrait-Head*, 1914 (fig. 23), and *Médrano I* and *II*. The neck, represented by a glass bottle painted on the inside and affixed to the torso at a right angle, as well as the painted wooden cones representing locks of hair, are very similar to those which appear in *Portrait-Head*, 1914. The shoulder, depicted schematically by means of a wooden plank, the cone-shaped breast, the convex conical torso, and the linear treatment of the fingers are all similar to their counterparts in *Médrano I (Juggler)*, 1912–1914 (illustrated p. 33, fig. 12), and *Médrano II (Dancer)*, 1914 (illustrated p. 26, fig. 7); the decorative lacelike motif representing a collar is also reminiscent of the one used on the edge of the skirt in *Médrano II*. The stylistic similarities between *Woman with Fan* and the three construc-

126

tions with which it has been compared here indicate that *Woman with Fan* may have gradually developed from these constructions (being one of the earliest of the sculpto-paintings). In his book, Archipenko himself included *Woman with Fan* among his constructions, defining it as a "construction—high relief."[90] Nevertheless, unlike *Médrano II*, which stands on a base joined at a right angle to the rear support, serving as a sort of niche enclosing the sculpture from the back, *Woman with Fan* has a framed, flat rear panel that supports and holds the composition, lending it the appearance of a "picture." It would thus seem more appropriate to define *Woman with Fan* as a sculpto-painting that may have developed from the constructions.

In *Woman with Fan*, painted illusionist details are added to the actual three-dimensional forms. An illusion of depth and the background perspective are achieved by the use of diagonal lines, shadows, and areas of various hues. The folds of the fan are illusionistically painted onto the bent sheet metal by means of shading. Archipenko's reference to pictorial conventions is reflected in this work not only in the combination of painting and sculpture, but also in the use of a canvas ground as the setting for his experiments.[91] It is interesting to compare the way the same subject is handled a year later in the sculpto-painting *Woman with Fan II*, 1915 (cat. no. 21). The compositional elements have become more compact and are situated closer to the background and there are more painted illusionist details: painted cylindrical forms appear beside an actual cylinder, and a breast, which looks three-dimensional, is painted beside a real cone representing the second breast.

Although the subject of *Woman with Fan* is a single figure, the use of assemblage to join its separate components gives the different spaces of the work a degree of independence. This is in contrast to Archipenko's treatment of space and composition in his modeled sculptures from the same year.

There is a greater sense of geometry in this sculpto-painting than in the modeled works. This difference in style is a result of the technique and the use of nonplastic materials, as Archipenko himself explained:

In this statue which I titled "Woman with Fan," and which dates 1914, I used a bottle to make the neck and sheet metal which I curved into a cone, to create the torso. The cone and the cylinder are the only shapes one can get from sheet metal through a simple intervention, without having to hammer the iron. To these shapes, in my statue, I added planks of wood. The final result is an ensemble of geometrical shapes, the geometry of which is a consequence of the materials used.[92]

Woman with Fan is depicted as a single, frontal, stylized figure, composed of physically separate schematized parts that are visually related in

Left: Fig. 24. Alexander Archipenko, *Woman with Fan*, 1914, before restoration.

Right: Fig. 25. *Woman with Fan*, after first stage of restoration, 1981. (Illustrated in color, page 15.)

a hieratic composition; it is painted in rich, warm, bold and glowing colors. These characteristics, as well as the inclusion of metal accessories in the painted surface, and the combination of paint and wood, suggest a possible source of inspiration in addition to cubism—the Russian icon.[93]

Sometime in the past, *Woman with Fan* suffered from damages. Unfortunately, the history of its condition, prior to its arrival in Tel Aviv, and during the early years of the museum, has not been recorded. The convex, cone-shaped breast and the lacelike collar have been lost. Where the convex cone had once been, a concave metal funnel remained (which originally served as the base for the breast), and nails were left where the collar had been joined. It would seem that perhaps in an attempt to repair early damage, the fan was moved some six centimeters to the left, together with the hand holding it (fig. 24).[94] In recent years, the work was compared with early photographs (among them one which appears in Archipenko's book, *Fifty Creative Years*),[95] and it became apparent that restoration and reconstruction work was needed.

The Tel Aviv Museum carried out this restoration and reconstruction in two stages. In the first stage, undertaken in 1981, the fan was returned to its original position and the hand readjusted accordingly (fig. 25). Yet, at that time, it was still not clear whether the other discrepancies resulted from damage to the work or whether the artist himself was involved with these alterations.

The second stage in the restoration, during which the breast and collar were reconstructed, was undertaken in 1986 when another early photograph was discovered. This came from the catalogue for the Grosse Berliner Kunstausstellung of 1926, where the sculpto-painting had been exhibited (cat. no. 10, pl. 2). In the 1926 reproduction, the breast and collar were still in their original position, although the fan had already been shifted. Since by this time Archipenko was in the United States (where he moved in 1923), it became clear that he was not responsible for changes in *Woman with Fan*, which took place only after 1926. Thus, these changes must have resulted from damage to the work and were not the artist's own modifications.

The sculpto-painting *Woman at Her Toilet (Woman before Mirror)*, 1916 (cat. no. 24), depicts a woman seated in an armchair before, or beside what might be a mirror, window, or doorway painted in linear perspective. The subject is represented by both painted and real forms: the legs are composed of painted metal, while the abdomen is painted so as to give the appearance of metal; the back of the armchair is similarly shown as a sinuous black line, and the armrests are represented by massive cylinders of real wood; half of the woman's face is flat—painted—the other half three-dimensional; one of the arms is painted with illusionistic depth, yet the other is sculpted; and two strips of wood form a real frame for an illusionary painted corridor of space representing the mirror or window.

Archipenko also called *Woman at Her Toilet*, "Woman Powdering Her Face,"[96] and in the early literature it is referred to as "Woman before a Mirror."[97] During the restoration work undertaken to remove rust stains from the sheet-metal panel on which the diagonal perspective lines are painted, the panel was detached, revealing a preparatory drawing of the woman's face (fig. 26). From this drawing it would appear that

the artist originally planned to include the woman's reflection in the mirror as he had done in at least three other works: *Before the Mirror (In the Boudoir)*, 1915 (cat. no. 20); *Woman before a Mirror*, 1915; and *Woman before Folding Mirror*, 1916. Whether real or painted, the mirror in the composition enabled Archipenko to play with illusion and reality and with optical tricks. Apparently, however, at a certain point in his work on *Woman at Her Toilet*, the artist became dissatisfied with the sketch of the woman's reflection in the mirror, or decided to replace it with a shiny metal surface, and so covered the mirror with sheet metal. Later, he painted the geometric areas of color conveying linear perspective on the metal, thus converting it into a doorway or window of the type often used by Italian Renaissance artists in painting interiors. Archipenko made use of this motif again a year later with the next sculpto-painting to be discussed, *Woman in Room*, 1917.

In *Woman in Room*, 1917 (cat. no. 26), Archipenko combined painting, assemblage, pen and ink drawing, and collage. Its central motif, constructed in wood and painted illusionistically, is a woman standing on a table or a pedestal. Adjacent to her on the table/pedestal, in reduced scale, is a still life—a vase on a table—drawn in pen and ink on paper, which is cut and pasted on the linen-covered wooden support. The contours of the small vase echo the curves of the female figure. This repetition of forms is a central element in the composition. It is interesting to note that a similar analogy between the female figure and a vase recurs in a series of works Archipenko created, culminating in *Vase Woman I* and *II*, both of 1919.

The female image, the subject of *Woman in Room*, could also be interpreted as a statue standing on a pedestal. This adds to the metaphysical ambiguity between painted and real form inherent in the medium of sculpto-painting. Actual three-dimensional objects—four pieces of wood representing the head, body, window, and table ledge—are juxtaposed with the painted conical shape representing the shoulders and torso, which from a distance appears more real than the actual projections. The head is also painted illusionistically on a flat piece of wood.[98] The composition is constructed of overlapping flat planes, both painted and real, placed parallel to the support.

Archipenko used the technique of collage as early as 1913 in preparatory studies that were related to his sculpture (*Figure*, 1913, cat. no. 9, *Figure in Movement*, 1913, cat. no. 8). The joining of diverse materials in the sculpto-painting was itself borrowed from the cubist collage. Yet, unlike the cubist collage, which often made use of found materials or chance discoveries, such as newspaper cutouts, wallpaper, or commercial labels, the collage in Archipenko's early studies, as well as in *Woman in Room*, consists of drawings on paper. The paper was cut with the same precision he had used to saw the wooden panels or cut the sheet metal for the sculpto-paintings.

The wooden support of *Woman in Room* is covered with linen coated with a very smooth, thick layer of gesso. The preparation of the support recalls the traditional technique by which the support for icons was produced. The smooth, shiny, enamellike effect that results, along with the bright and contrasting colors and the geometric and stylized composition in this work, may reflect the influence of Russian icons.

The fourth sculpto-painting in the Goeritz Collection, *Kneeling Woman*, 1916–1917 (cat. no. 25), illustrates the next stage of Archipenko's development in this unique medium. One of the innovations in this work is the extension of the three-dimensional figure beyond the support and the frame, at the top. The projection of the head and the elliptical panel behind it are also reminiscent of Russian icons in which,

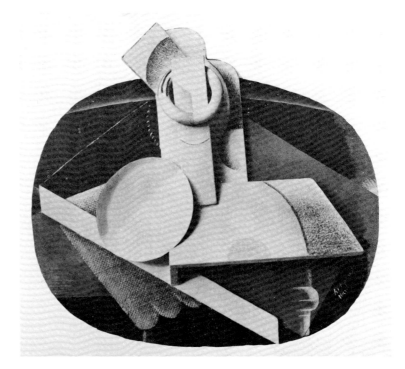

more than once, the Madonna's head and halo extend beyond the perimeters of the frame. Other elements of the composition project forward from the background.

In comparison with the three previously discussed sculpto-paintings, in which illusionist effects play a major role in depicting the subject and background, adding to the complexity of the composition, the composition of *Kneeling Woman* is more abstract. The painted effects, schematic and mostly nonillusionistic, play a minor role in the composition. The background is relatively flat, with no perspective. In *Kneeling Woman* it is the sculpted relief and play of actual light and shadow that are of primary interest. The relief is of one material only—wood—and is constructed of superimposed, flat geometric layers.

The female figure—the subject of this piece—has been broken up into its component parts, which are rearranged as in synthetic cubism. They are painted schematically or represented by actual three-dimensional geometric wooden pieces: a sphere or semi-sphere (the breasts); a round disk (the heel); a wooden ring cut in half (the head); a rectangular wooden panel (the torso); and a half-cylinder (the arm). Due to the building up of layers, the view from the side is particularly interesting and is important; Archipenko included in his composition the profile of the figure which can only be perceived from the side.

The colors used in *Kneeling Woman* are totally unlike those in the three previous sculpto-paintings. Whereas the former were bright and

Fig. 27. Alexander Archipenko, *Head and Still Life*, 1916, painted wood, metal, and canvas, location unknown (from *Alexander Archipenko, Fifty Creative Years*).

OPPOSITE PAGE
Fig. 28. Alexander Archipenko, *Standing Figure*, 1917, painted wood and painted sheet metal, location unknown (from *Alexander Archipenko, Fifty Creative Years*).

132

multicolored, in this work the dominant colors are subdued, earth tones with the addition of white and green.

The composition, which is more in the spirit of synthetic cubism, the simple, clearly defined geometric forms, the flat background, the substitution of schematic lines for painted illusionist elements, the overlapping planes, and the radical change in the color scale indicate that *Kneeling Woman* was executed at a later stage in Archipenko's development and not in 1914, a date formerly ascribed to it in the 1981 catalogue.[99] Stylistically, *Kneeling Woman* resembles two other sculpto-paintings by Archipenko—*Head and Still Life*, 1916 (fig. 27), and *Standing Figure*, 1917 (fig. 28). Although one painted illusionistic element—a carved table leg—does appear in *Head and Still Life*, the rest of the composition is abstract and geometric and is constructed of overlapping flat surfaces. The head and the surface behind it extend beyond the perimeters of the supporting panel, and the head is represented by a wooden ring similar to the one in *Kneeling Woman. Standing Figure* does not contain any painted illusionistic elements whatsoever. The composition is geometric, abstract, and constructivist. The head is again represented by a wooden ring, and locks of hair are schematically shown as sinuous lines; both elements are like those in *Kneeling Woman.*

Like most of Archipenko's sculpto-paintings, *Kneeling Woman* was executed in Nice, as indicated by the artist's signature: "Archipenko/ Nice." The only early bibliographical source for the date of this work is Maurice Raynal (1923) who dates it 1917.[100] On the basis of Raynal's dating and the above stylistic comparisons, we may conclude that the work was produced in Nice in 1916/1917, rather than in 1914.

In early 1920, Archipenko created his two largest sculpto-paintings: *Woman*, produced in Paris (Tel Aviv Museum, cat. no. 31), and *Two Women*, produced in Zurich (National Museum, Belgrade, cat. no. 32).[101] *Woman*, a sheet-metal construction on a panel covered with burlap, is the taller of the two (1.87 meters high). It is a monumental piece, the culmination of a series of works on the theme of the female figure. Archipenko showed it in the last exhibition of the Section d'Or group, held in Galerie La Boétie in Paris in March 1920. It was displayed on the balcony of the gallery, not far from Léger's *La Ville*, 1919.[102] The profound impression it made there is apparent from the description of the critic Iwan Goll:

This figure in bright metal stood in the center of the hall one afternoon while a concert was going on, high above the wave of black tuxedos, white faces, and brown violins, and on its facets and curves it brought to life, a thousand times

Fig. 29. Alexander Archipenko, *Woman*, 1919, painted wood, sheet metal, and metal tubing on oil on burlap, The Tel Aviv Museum, The Erich Goeritz Collection.

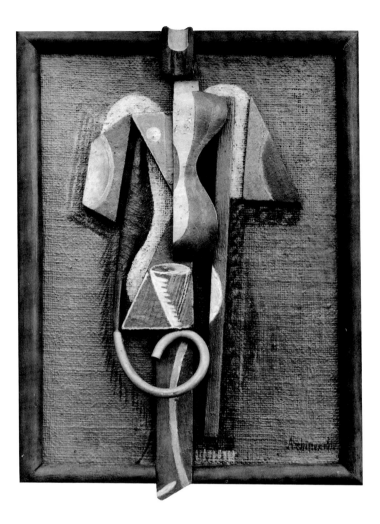

over, every movement of the musicians and the audience, attracting more attention than even the conductor himself. Like a huge diamond this central work reflected each external sparkle in all the variations of the rainbow colors. It seemed as if some internal window was opening out to the world here, allowing events of unknown horizons to enter in.[103]

In the same year (1920), *Woman* was shown in Archipenko's exhibition held in the Russian pavilion at the Venice Biennale. Although it was sold to Falk in Geneva at the end of that year, Archipenko sent a photograph of the work to Marcel Duchamp to be included in the catalogue of the Archipenko exhibition organized by the Société Anonyme in New York in 1921. A reproduction of the work appeared on the back cover of the catalogue,[104] indicating that Archipenko considered it of particular importance.

Woman, 1919 (fig. 29), also at the Tel Aviv Museum, is apparently the smallest of the sculpto-paintings created by Archipenko. Donald Karshan considers it a study for the larger *Woman*, of 1920. He sees a similarity between the two sculpto-paintings in their central axis and the frontality of the composition, and in the extremities—head and feet—extending beyond the picture frame. The two works also have the same relatively simple neutral background, oil paint on burlap. In the larger work of 1920, Archipenko elongated the proportions of the female image and simplified and reduced the composition. The coiled metal tube in the smaller work was eliminated so as not to interrupt the flow of the basic form. Whereas in the smaller work the image consists of pieces of wood, sheet metal, and metal tubes, here it has been transformed into polished metal set against a simpler and even more neutral background.[105]

The use of polished metal, reflective of its surroundings, carried Archipenko's spatial conception a step further, leading to a dematerialization of matter. As early as 1914, Archipenko had used highly polished surfaces for their reflective quality *(Portrait-Head)*, but it was not until after the war that he used it again to enhance the optical effect of interchanging convex and concave forms under certain lighting conditions,[106] as he did with *Woman*.

Of the sculpto-paintings chosen for the current exhibition, three are characterized by a complex composition combining painted illusionistic elements with concrete three-dimensional forms and by the use of bold colors. The other two, representing a later approach, are marked by a relative simplicity, clarity of composition and background, a more schematic presentation of the subject, and subdued colors, with a greater emphasis on three-dimensional sculptural aspects rather than on illusionist painting.

The discussion of Archipenko's works in the Goeritz Collection has demonstrated that even before the influence of cubism became apparent in Archipenko's work, there existed a certain degree of anatomical reduction and a geometric element in his compositions, even when the stance and proportions of the figure recalled classical models. Already at an early stage in his work the dismembered "partial figure" became part of the process of formal reduction, hand-in-hand with a new perception of space-mass relationships. At the same time, the modeled sculpture reflected a new interrelationship between the figure and its base.

The influence of cubism, first seen in the collection in a work from 1913, was initially expressed in the simultaneous viewing of the object from a number of vantage points and in the fragmentation of the sculpted surfaces into facets. Later, it was found in the optical effects

135

possible with a reversal between convex and concave forms and in the substitution of void for mass.

Along with these innovations, still executed in conventional techniques and materials, Archipenko was experimenting with polychromed sculpture, the technique of assemblage, and the incorporation of nontraditional materials. In the sculpto-paintings, he combined such materials as wood, sheet metal, glass, ready-made objects, oilcloth, and burlap, as well as reflective polished metal.

The collection clearly reflects the diversity of Archipenko's oeuvre as well as the imagination, boldness, and quest for formal innovations that characterized his artistic development in Europe.

TRANSLATED BY SARA KITAI

Notes

In the course of my research on the history of the Goeritz Collection at the Tel Aviv Museum, I obtained much new and valuable information, both in conversation and in the form of documentary material from scholars, colleagues, and members of the Goeritz family. I wish to take this opportunity to express my gratitude to all of them.

Valuable information concerning the collector S. G. Falk was generously shared by Susanne Schiller of Heidelberg University. The resources and efficient staffs of the following archives provided me with research materials: The Kunsthalle Mannheim Archives, with the assistance of Manfred Fath and Roland Dorn; the Archives of American Art in New York; and Tami Freiman at the Tel Aviv Museum Archives. Several people were generous with their time, granting me interviews or corresponding with me. In this regard, I would like to mention Andrew Goeritz and Rachel Goeritz Pollack, Manfred Lehmbruck, and Eva Spector.

I am indebted to Donald Karshan, Katherine Michaelsen, and Margit Rowell for the scholarly advice and useful information they provided me in the course of researching Archipenko's works in the Tel Aviv Museum collection.

1. During the war, a number of Archipenko's sculptures were stored in a shed in Paris, while the artist himself was living in Nice. These works were damaged as a result of severe water leakage. Other works were destroyed by air raids during World War I in Paris as well as in Hagen, Germany, when the local museum was demolished.

2. Letter from Archipenko to Karl Schwarz, 9 May 1947, in the Tel Aviv Museum Archives. During the 1940s, after the war, Archipenko started writing his book (published only in 1960). He was looking, at that time, for his early works, which had been left in Europe. It was Mrs. Irmi Selver, the sister-in-law of Mr. Goeritz, who informed Archipenko of the Goeritz Collection at the Tel Aviv Museum.

3. Alexander Archipenko and Fifty Art Historians, *Archipenko, Fifty Creative Years, 1908–1958* (New York, 1960), caption to pl. 141.

4. Letter from Archipenko to Haim Gamzu, 27 July 1947, in the Tel Aviv Museum Archives.

5. This research was done by Edna Moshenson, curator of prints and drawings, the Tel Aviv Museum.

6. Katherine J. Michaelsen, *Archipenko, A Study of the Early Works* 1908-1920 (New York, 1977), 135. Michaelsen writes: "the brother of George Falk, Sally Falk, was also an important collector and patron of Wilhelm Lehmbruck. There are portraits of Mr. & Mrs. Sally Falk by the German sculptor." This information is based on a letter from Reinhold Heller to Katherine J. Michaelsen, dated 5 May 1974, in which Heller informed Michaelsen that ". . . Herr *Sally* Falk was Lehmbruck's patron . . . his collection, sold following his bankruptcy in 1919, contained no Archipenko sculpture. The George (Georg?) Falk who did collect Archipenko's work was Sally Falk's brother. . . ." This information, in turn, was acquired by checking with the Lehmbrucks and the Kunsthalle Mannheim. In a letter from *Kunstarchiv Arntz* (Wilhelm F. Arntz) to Andrew Goeritz (undated, in reply to a letter from Goeritz to Arntz, dated 21 August 1980) the two brothers are mentioned again. Arntz wrote: "I knew the collector Falk from Mannheim, who may be the brother of George Falk from Geneva, very superficially during my years in Frankfurt (prior to 1933). The sculptor Wilhelm Lehmbruck made several portraits of him and his wife. . . ."

7. Susanne Schiller, *Sally Falks Stiftung von Plastiken an die Mannheimer Kunsthalle* (Heidelberg, 1985).

8. According to a document issued by the Städtisches Archiv, Mannheim, on 24 April 1961, Sally Falk was born in Heilbronn on 22 March 1888, the only son of Felix Falk, born in Braunsbach, 14 March 1857. This document is in the Kunsthalle Mannheim Archives, Sally Falk File (hereafter referred to as "K.M.A., S.F.F.").

9. Städtisches Archiv, Mannheim.

10. Städtisches Archiv, Mannheim, and also Lothar Fischer, *George Grosz* (Hamburg, 1976), 43; George Grosz, *Ein Kleines Ja und ein Grosses Nein* (Hamburg, 1955), 107.

11. Falk was a patron of George Grosz. As Grosz related in his memoirs, at a certain point Falk offered him a monthly allowance (Grosz 1955, 107), but the arrangement never materialized and Falk's patronage did not last more than a year (compare Fischer 1976, 43).

12. Grosz 1955, 107–108, 186–187.

13. Letter from Falk to Hartlaub, 20 February 1918 (K.M.A., S.F.F.).

14. Paul Westheim, "Erinnerung an eine Sammlung," in *Das Kunstblatt* (1918), no. 8, 233–241. This article does not specify the name of the collector but rather discusses a collection that no longer exists. I wish to thank Roland Dorn, of the Kunsthalle Mannheim, for bringing this article to my attention.

15. Schiller 1985, 14–15.

16. Letter from Hartlaub to Weichert, 10 January 1917 (K.M.A., S.F.F.).

17. According to Reinhold Heller, *The Art of Wilhelm Lehmbruck* [exh. cat., National Gallery of Art] (Washington, 1972), 181. In 1916 Lehmbruck sought to leave Germany for Switzerland, to escape military duty during World War I. He moved to Zurich. In January 1917, he cabled his family in Berlin to accompany the Falk family to Zurich immediately. The friendship between the two families remained close in Switzerland; when the Falks were staying in hotels and a sanatorium in Arosa, Lehmbruck visited them. Two portraits of Falk by Lehmbruck, dated 1916, are drawn on paper bearing the letterhead: Hotel Valsaua, Arosa. The drawings are reproduced in Gerhard Händler, *Wilhelm Lehmbruck—Drawings from the Mature Period* (Stuttgart, 1985), 157. Also, compare Dietrich Schubert, *Die Kunst Lehmbrucks* (Worms, 1981), 213.

18. Letter from Hartlaub to customs office, 15 November 1917 (K.M.A., S.F.F.).

19. Letter from Manfred Lehmbruck to Nehama Guralnik, 15 February 1986.

20. Schiller 1985, 11.

21. Grosz 1955, 107.

22. The following were exhibited in the Wilhelm Lehmbruck exhibition at the National Gallery of Art, Washington in 1972: *Portrait of Herr Falk*, 1915–1916 (stone, Collection Wilhelm Lehmbruck Museum, Duisburg); *Portrait of Herr Falk*, 1915 (bronze, Collection Mr. & Mrs. J. H. Guttmann, New York); *Portrait Bust of Frau Falk*, 1915–1916 (red stone, Collection Family of the artist); *Portrait Bust of Frau Falk*, 1915–1916 (bronze, Collection Mr. & Mrs. J. H. Guttmann, New York); *Portrait Bust of Frau Falk*, 1915–1916 (marble, Collection Wilhelm Lehmbruck Museum, Duisburg); *Portrait Statuette of Frau Falk*, 1915–1916 (bronze, Collection Wilhelm Lehmbruck Museum, Duisburg).

23. *Portrait of Mr. F.*, 1915–1916 (bronze); *Portrait Statuette of Mrs. Falk*, 1915–1916 (terra-cotta); and *Head of the Rising Youth*, 1913 (cast stone) were also gifts of the Goeritz family, 1955.

24. Schubert 1981, 214.

25. According to Douglas Lewis, curator of sculpture at the National Gallery of Art, Washington, the following is the provenance for *Seated Youth (The Friend)*, 1917 (fig. 13): Purchased by Sally Falk from the artist, 1917; on loan to the Kunsthalle Mannheim, 1917-1921; gift by Falk to the Kunsthalle Mannheim, 1921; confiscated by the Nazis from the Kunsthalle Mannheim, 1937; purchased by Curt Valentin, through the Buchholz Gallery, c. 1938, from above source; acquired by Walter Chrysler, 1939, from Valentin; acquired by Claus Virsch, 1971, from Chrysler; sold by Virsch to National Gallery of Art, Washington, 1974.

26. *Kneeling Woman*, 1911, was also confiscated from the Kunsthalle Mannheim; it was acquired in 1939 through the Abby Aldrich Rockefeller Fund for the Museum of Modern Art, New York.

27. *Seated Youth (The Friend)*, 1917; *Kneeling Woman*, 1911 (cast stone, figs. 14 and 15); *Torso of a Young Girl*, 1914 (cast stone); *Bust of a Woman (Mrs. L.)*, 1910–1911 (bronze); *The Contemplative One*, 1910–1911 (terra-cotta statuette); and *Seated Girl*, 1913–1914 (bronze).

28. *Athlete*, 1912–1913, by Edwin Scharff; *Slave*, 1916, by Georg Kolbe; and *Boy*, 1911,

by Ernesto di Fiori. Schiller 1985, 31–39, 48–54.

29. For notarized agreement, dated 28 March 1917, and list of basis of the Falk loan, see Schiller 1985, Appendices VI (b) (e).

30. Cable from Hartlaub to Falk, 25 February 1918 (K.M.A., S.F.F.).

31. Letter from Falk to Hartlaub, 20 February 1918 (K.M.A., S.F.F.).

32. Attachment order, 22 January 1919, against Sally Falk.

33. Letterhead on his letters in 1918: Sanatorium Altein, Arosa.

34. Attachment order, 22 January 1919, against Sally Falk for debt of M 172,000 (K.M.A., S.F.F.).

35. Schiller 1985, 20.

36. Sale contract dated 6 January 1919.

37. Correspondence between Neumann and Kunsthalle Mannheim concerning sale of Sally Falk Collection (K.M.A., S.F.F.).

38. In a letter, dated 12 May 1919, Falk announces his intention to stay in Geneva, and as of August 1919, his permanent address in Geneva is on his letterhead: Maison Royale, Quai des Eaux Vives.

39. Letter from Manfred Lehmbruck to Nehama Guralnik, 15 February 1986.

40. Schiller 1985, 13.

41. Michaelsen 1977, 19.

42. Eva Spector in a conversation with Nehama Guralnik, Tel Aviv, 26 January 1986.

43. Letter from Lehmbruck to Guralnik, 15 February 1986, and letter from Reinhold Heller to Katherine Michaelsen, 5 May 1974.

44. Lists of sales to J. B. Neumann and Paul Cassirer (K.M.A., S.F.F.).

45. According to Archipenko (Archipenko 1960), the G. Falk Collection included at least three works which were not in the Goeritz Collection: *Bather*, 1915 (cat. no. 23); *Woman with Umbrella/Silhouette*, 1913; and *Still Life*, 1920.

46. At least eight works from the Falk Collection were exhibited at the Kundig Bookshop. Four of them are listed as belonging to a Swiss collection (marked *): 7. *Kneeling Woman*, 1910 (cat. no. 2); 23c. *Kneeling Woman*, 1916–1917 (cat. no. 25); 15a/b. *Statuette*, 1915 (cat. no. 19); 1a. *Walking Soldier*, 1917 (cat. no. 27); *Woman in Room*, 1917 (cat. no. 26); 19. *Woman*, 1918; 22/23. *Woman in Armchair*, 1918; 20. *Woman*, 1919.

47. Elie Faure (preface), *Exposition Internationale d'Art Moderne*, (Geneva, 26 December 1920–25 January 1921).

48. Letter in the Société Anonyme Collection at the Beinecke Rare Book and Manuscript Library, Yale University. I am grateful to Katherine Michaelsen for this information.

49. The following works from the Falk Collection were included in the 1920–1921 exhibition in Geneva: 30. *Leaning Woman* (cat. no. 13); 17. *Bather* (cat. no. 4); 24. *Repose* (titled: *Femme couchée*) (cat. no. 5); 27. *Kneeling Woman* (titled: *Accroupie*) (cat. no. 2); 16. *Woman at Her Toilet* (cat. no. 24); 23. *Woman*; 19. *Seated Woman* (cat. no. 29).

50. According to Theodor Däubler and Iwan Goll, *Archipenko Album* (Potsdam, 1921), in 1921, the following works were already in a private collection (the name of the collector was not specified): 7. *Woman with Fan* (cat. no. 17); 22. *Statuette* (cat. no. 19); 26. *Walking Soldier* (cat. no. 27); 27. *Woman* (cat. no. 31). Since we know that Archipenko sold *Woman* to Falk, we may assume that he was the private collector of these works.

Also in Hans Hildebrandt, *Alexandre Archipenko: Son Oeuvre* (Berlin, 1923), four works are listed as belonging to the Falk Collection: 19. *Statue on a Triangular Base Statuette* (cat. no. 15); 49. *Woman at Her Toilet* (titled: *Femme au Miroir*) (cat. no. 24); 61. *Woman*; 13. *Seated Woman* (cat. no. 29). Another work is listed as belonging to a private collection: 54. *Woman*. From this information, we may conclude that Falk had already collected a considerable number of works by Archipenko by as early as 1920 and continued to do so during the early 1920s.

51. Letter from Falk to the Kunsthalle Mannheim, 2 February 1961 (K.M.A., S.F.F.).

52. Schiller 1985, 21.

53. Letter from Mayor of Mannheim to Falk (K.M.A., S.F.F.).

54. Schiller 1985, 21.

55. Andrew Goeritz, in conversation with Nehama Guralnik, London, 7 February 1986.

56. Erich Goeritz' biography from Edna Moshenson, "Erich Goeritz—The Collector," *Archipenko, The Early Works: 1910–1921* [exh. cat., Tel Aviv Museum] (Tel Aviv, 1981), as well as the Erich Goeritz file, Tel Aviv Museum Archives.

57. Letter from Goeritz to Schwarz, in the Tel Aviv Museum Archives.

58. Letter from Goeritz to Eugene Kolb, 28 February 1955, in the Tel Aviv Museum Archives.

59. Werner Hofmann, *The Sculpture of Henri Laurens* (New York, 1970), 11.

60. Michaelsen 1977, 13.

61. Albert Elsen, *The Partial Figure in Modern Sculpture from Rodin to 1969* (Baltimore, 1970); Albert Elsen, *Origins of Modern Sculpture: Pioneers and Premises* (New York, 1974), 73–79.

62. Elsen 1974, 76.

63. Elsen 1974, 119.

64. Bernard Dorival, "Les Omissions d'Archipenko et Lipchitz," *Bulletin de la Société de l'Histoire de l'Art Français* (1974), 206, pl. 36/37.

65. Hildebrandt 1923, 9.

66. Dorival 1974, 204, pl. 15/16.

67. Roland Schacht, "Alexander Archipenko," *Sturm Album II* (Berlin, 1924), 10.

68. Dorival 1974, 204; Michaelsen 1977, 31.

69. Michaelsen 1977, 30–31.

70. Elsen 1974, 114.

71. Donald Karshan, *Archipenko, The Early Works: 1910–1921* [exh. cat., The Tel Aviv Museum] (Tel Aviv, 1981), cat. no. 4.

72. According to Michaelsen (Michaelsen 1977, 60), the artist's widow, Frances Archipenko, recalls Archipenko speaking of architectural embellishments he worked on in Kiev while he was a student there, but no trace of these has survived.

73. Among the artists who met in Puteaux were Raymond Duchamp-Villon, Jacques Villon, Marcel Duchamp, Albert Gleizes, Jean Metzinger, Fernand Léger, Henri Le Fauconnier, Juan Gris, Roger de La Fresnaye, Francis Picabia, and Robert Delaunay. For further information, see William Camfield, "La Section d'Or," in *Albert Gleizes and the Section d'Or* [exh. cat., Leonard Hutton Galleries] (New York, 1964); and Michaelsen 1970, 60–61.

74. William C. Agee, "Notes on the Sculptures," in *Raymond Duchamp-Villon 1879–1918* (New York, 1967), 65–79.

75. George Heard Hamilton, "Raymond Duchamp-Villon," in *Raymond Duchamp-Villon 1879–1918* (New York, 1967), 20.

76. Der Sturm Gallery (Berlin, September 1913).

77. Eva Spector in a conversation with Nehama Guralnik.

78. Archipenko 1960, pl. 77.

79. *Leaning Woman* is dated 1911 by Archipenko in *Fifty Creative Years* (pl. 77). Its reproduction appears in the book adjacent to that of a bronze statue, *Negro Dancer,* also dated 1911 (pl. 76). Donald Karshan (Karshan 1981, no. 2) dated the work 1911, adopting the date given by the artist. Karshan regarded the juxtaposition of the two works as further proof that Archipenko himself linked the two together. Michaelsen (Michaelsen 1977, 99–102) dates the work 1913–1914. She rejects the latter argument, claiming that the two works are very dissimilar. She points out that *Negro Dancer* is a relatively realistic figure; although some of the limbs are missing, the female figure is depicted in detail, including the breast, curves of the hips, thighs, and knees. In contrast, the female form in *Leaning Woman* is only implied; its anatomy is abstract and drastically reduced to a series of conical and tubular forms with no treatment of details.

Yet, *Leaning Woman,* as Michaelsen notes, shows a similarity to some of Archipenko's later works. The treatment of the neck and shoulders joined in one unit—shaped like a conical funnel—is similar to that in the previously discussed sculpture, *Statue on Triangular Base (Statuette),* 1914 (cat. no. 15). In both works, as well, the silhouette of

Fig. 30. Alexander Archipenko, *Woman with Umbrella/Silhouette*, 1913, bronze, location unknown (from *Alexander Archipenko, Fifty Creative Years*). (Discussed in note 79.)

the body is relatively slender, reduced to geometric elements, with the surface broken up into facets. Michaelsen suggests that *Leaning Woman* is a simplified and more abstract version of *Red Dance*, 1912–1913 (illustrated p. 22, fig. 2). The arched pose of the body and the artist's attempt to enclose the space by means of the mass of the arched figure is similar in both. Furthermore (as Michaelsen notes in a letter, 11 September 1985), *Leaning Woman* bears a resemblance to *Woman with Umbrella/Silhouette*, 1913 (fig. 30), in terms of the level of abstraction and the lack of adherance to anatomical detail. Both were originally produced in gilded plaster. According to Michaelsen, a photograph in the archives of the artist's estate shows gilded plaster versions of the two sculptures adjacent to each other. She notes that the only other works that Archipenko is known to have produced in gilded plaster are *Hero*, 1913, and *Flat Torso*, 1914.

All of the stylistic evidence mentioned above seems to indicate that *Leaning Woman* belongs to a stage in the artist's development in which he was already retreating from compact archaic compositions and probing the question of the interrelationship between mass and the surrounding space, as well as allowing himself greater freedom in interpreting anatomical features. The catalogue of the Archipenko exhibition in Der Sturm Gallery in Berlin in 1921 is the only early source for the 1913 date, which appears more reasonable than the one given by the artist himself (1911). Because of its stylistic similarity to the works produced in 1913/1914, the date for *Leaning Woman* has been revised to 1913–1914.

80. Archipenko 1960, 56–58.

81. Michaelsen 1977, 98.

82. Michaelsen 1977, 98.

83. Theodor Däubler, who was Falk's friend and knew him and his wife well, wrote of this work: ". . . Also a success is an abstract double portrait which is in color and simultaneously has a strong play of light and shade (as it is architecture). The likeness with the represented couple is masterfully achieved! The mobility of both people was stylistically brought to the deepest inner stillness. Rhythms lead from reality to truth. It is a special achievement!" (Theodor Däubler, Introduction, *Archipenko Album* [Potsdam, 1921], 10.)

84. Grosz 1955, 107.

85. *Standing Woman (Mrs. Falk)*, 1920, wax on wood base, 36 cm (h.), signed, dated, and inscribed: *Archipenko à Madame Falk 1920 Genève*.

86. Michaelsen 1977, 136.

87. Michaelsen 1977, 84–85.

88. Katherine Kuh, *Alexander Archipenko* [exh. cat., UCLA Art Galleries] (Los Angeles, 1967), 8.

89. If we consider *Médrano II*, 1914 (The Solomon R. Guggenheim Museum, New York), as a construction, rather than a sculpto-painting.

90. Archipenko 1960, 65.

91. Margit Rowell, *The Planar Dimension* [exh. cat., The Solomon R. Guggenheim Museum] (New York, 1979), 18.

92. Yvon Taillandier, "Conversations avec Archipenko," in *XXᵉ Siecle*, no. 22 (1963).

93. Karshan 1981, no. 10; Rowell 1979, 18–19.

94. During the restoration of this work at the Tel Aviv Museum, upon removing the fan and returning it to its original position, a crumpled piece of newspaper, supporting the fan in place, was discovered. It was a piece from the *Journal de Genève*, dated 21 September 1919. One may conclude, therefore, that the fan was damaged and affixed to its new position in Geneva not earlier than September 1919.

95. Archipenko 1960, pl. 65.

96. Archipenko, 1960, pl. 56.

97. Erich Wiese, "Alexander Archipenko," in *Junge Kunst*, vol. 40 (Leipzig, 1923), pl. xxiv; Hans Hildebrandt, *Alexandre Archipenko: Son Oeuvre* (Berlin, 1923), pl. 49.

98. The original head was lost sometime in the past; the present head was reconstructed at the Tel Aviv Museum according to photographs (see Archipenko 1960, pl. 48).

99. Originally, the work was dated 1914–1918 at the Tel Aviv Museum. In 1981, Donald Karshan dated it 1914 (Karshan 1981, no. 11). Michaelsen (Michaelsen 1977,

137–138) dated the work 1918–1919 because of stylistic considerations and also taking into account the date 1919, given in Archipenko's estate archives.

100. Maurice Raynal, A. *Archipenko* (Rome, 1923), no. 25.

101. *Woman*, 1920, is signed, lower right: Archipenko/Paris. *Two Women* is signed and is dated: Zurich, I.1920.

102. Karshan 1981, no. 24.

103. Däubler and Goll 1921, 14.

104. Archipenko exhibition, Société Anonyme Inc. (New York, 1 February-15 March, 1921).

105. Karshan 1981, no. 23.

106. Elsen 1974, 112.

CATALOGUE

1

Sorrow (Tristesse)
(1909)
painted wood
9½ (24) h.

Provenance

From the artist

Madame Jean G. Verdier, Cannes, France, 1921–1966

Joseph H. Hirshhorn, New York, 1966–1972

Hirshhorn Museum and Sculpture Garden, Smithsonian Institution, Washington

2

Kneeling Woman
(1910)
bronze
13¼ (30) h.

Provenance

From the artist

Probably S.G. Falk, Geneva

Erich Goeritz, Berlin, until 1933

On loan to the Tel Aviv Museum from
Erich Goeritz, 1933–1956

Private Collection, London

3

Mother and Child
(1910–1911)
marble
13½ (34.7) h.
signed: *Archipenko*

Provenance
Galerie Flechtheim (?), Berlin
Grandfather of present owner, Berlin,
1920s

Private Collection

4

Bather (Seated Woman)
1912
terra-cotta
17¼ (44) h.
signed: *Archipenko 1912*

Provenance

From the artist

Probably S.G. Falk, Geneva

Erich Goeritz, Berlin, until 1933

On loan to the Tel Aviv Museum from
Erich Goeritz, 1933–1956

The Tel Aviv Museum, Gift of the
Goeritz Family, London, 1956

5

Repose

1912
plaster tinted pink
14⅛ x 5⅜ (36 x 39)
signed: *Archipenko 1912*

Provenance

From the artist

Probably S.G. Falk, Geneva

Erich Goeritz, Berlin, until 1933

On loan to the Tel Aviv Museum from
Erich Goeritz, 1933–1956

The Tel Aviv Museum, Gift of the
Goeritz Family, London, 1956

6

Porteuse (Bearer)
(1912)
stone
17½ (45) h.
signed: *Archipenko*

Provenance
Galerie Maeght, Paris, c. 1954
Private Collection, Belgium
Perls Galleries, New York, 1984

Donald Karshan Collection, Florida

Madonna of the Rocks

1912

plaster painted red

21 (53.2) h.

signed: *Archipenko/1912*

Provenance

From the artist

Fernand Léger

Alexander Archipenko and Klaus Perls
(from Nadia Léger)

The Museum of Modern Art, New York,
Gift of Frances Archipenko Gray and
Perls Galleries, 1969

NGA only

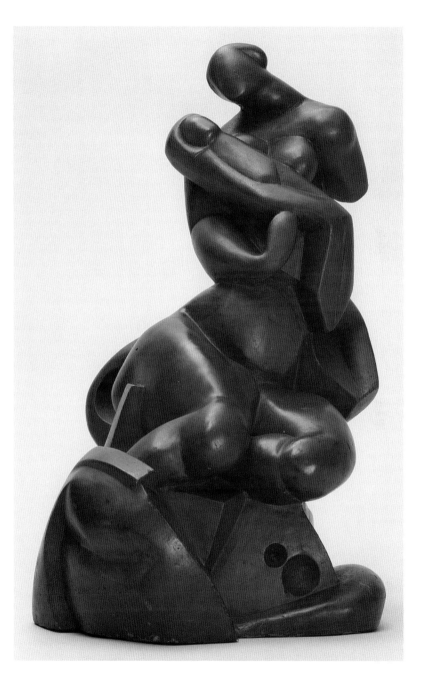

Figure in Movement
1913
cut and pasted papers, crayon, and pencil
18¾ x 12⅜ (47.6 x 31.4)
signed: *Archipenko/Paris* 1913

The Museum of Modern Art, New York,
Gift of Perls Galleries, New York

NGA only

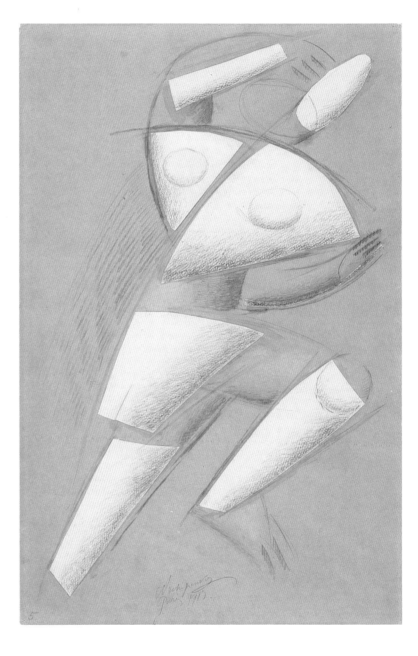

9

Figure
(1913)
collage, pencil, and pastel
18¾ x 12¼ (47.7 x 31.3)

Provenance

Galerie Jean Chauvelin, Paris

Perls Galleries, New York, 1974

Donald Karshan Collection, Florida

Collage: Two Figures
1913
gouache and pasted paper
18¾ x 12⅜ (47.5 x 31.5)
signed: A. *Archipenko/Paris 1913*

Provenance
Nell Walden, 1958

Moderna Museet, Stockholm

11

Composition (Composition: Two Figures)
1913
collage, pen and ink
18¾ x 12¼ (47.7 x 31.3)
signed: *Archipenko/1913*

The Museum of Modern Art, New York, Extended loan from Frances Archipenko Gray

NGA only

12

Sketch for Ceiling
1913
plaster
19¹¹/₁₆ x 12⅝ x 5⁵/₁₆ (50 x 55 x 13.5)
signed, lower right: *Archipenko Paris 1913*

Provenance

Galerie Der Sturm, Berlin

Eva Spector, Berlin, 1925–1929, Tel Aviv from 1929

Sam and Ayala Zacks, Toronto

The Tel Aviv Museum, Gift of Mrs. Ayala Zacks-Abramov, 1983

TAM only

13

Leaning Woman (Penché)
(1913–1914)
polished bronze
11½ (29) h.

Provenance

From the artist

Probably S.G. Falk, Geneva

Erich Goeritz, Berlin, until 1933

On loan to the Tel Aviv Museum from
Erich Goeritz, 1933–1956

The Tel Aviv Museum, Gift of the
Goeritz Family, London, 1956

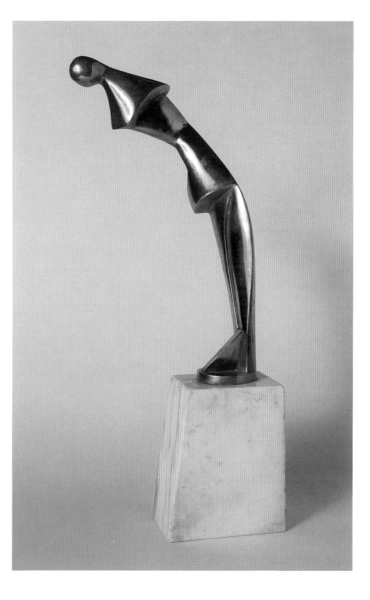

14

Boxing (Boxers, Struggle)
1914
plaster painted black
23¾ (60. 3) h.
signed: A. Archipenko/Paris 1914

Provenance
From the artist
Alberto Magnelli, Florence, 1914–1955

The Solomon R. Guggenheim
Museum, New York

NGA only

15

Statue on Triangular Base
(Statuette)
1914
plaster
31¼ (79.5) h.
signed: *Archipenko 1914*

Provenance

From the artist

S.G. Falk, Geneva

Erich Goeritz, Berlin, until 1933

On loan to the Tel Aviv Museum from
Erich Goeritz, 1933–1956

The Tel Aviv Museum, Gift of the
Goeritz Family, London, 1956

16

Geometric Statuette

1914
plaster
20½ (52.5) h.
signed: *Archipenko 1914*

Provenance

From the artist

Probably S.G. Falk, Geneva

Erich Goeritz, Berlin

On loan to the Tel Aviv Museum from
Erich Goeritz

Erich Goeritz, London

On loan from Eric and Salome
Estorick

Woman with Fan

1914

painted wood, painted sheet metal,
glass bottle, and metal funnel; support:
oil on burlap, and oil on oilcloth,
mounted on wood panels

42½ x 24¼ x 5 (108 x 61.5 x 13.5)

signed, lower right: A. *Archipenko*/ *1914*

Provenance

From the artist

S.G. Falk Collection, Geneva

Erich Goeritz, Berlin, until 1933

On loan to the Tel Aviv Museum from
Erich Goeritz, 1933–1956

The Tel Aviv Museum, Gift of the
Goeritz Family, London, 1956

18

Flat Torso
(1915)
marble on alabaster base
18¾ (47.6) h.
signed: *Archipenko*

Provenance

C.S.L. Trask, London, 1926–1957

Sotheby and Co., London, 1957

Marlborough Fine Art, Ltd., 1958

Galerie des Arts Anciens et Modernes,
Schaan, Liechtenstein

Joseph H. Hirshhorn, New York,
1958–1966

Hirshhorn Museum and Sculpture
Garden, Smithsonian Institution,
Washington

NGA only (illustrated)

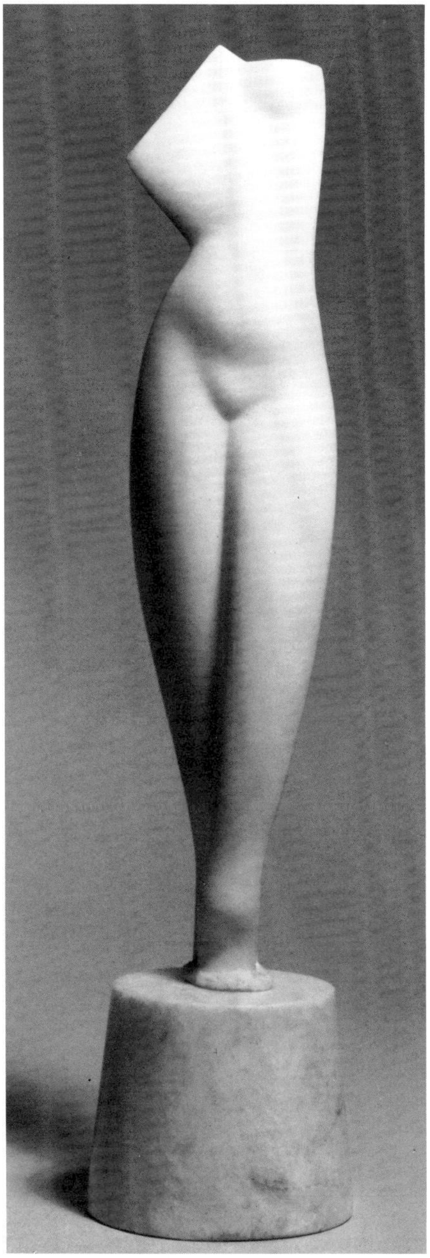

Flat Torso
(1914)
plaster
15⅜ (39) h. without base
signed: *Archipenko*

Provenance

From the artist

Probably S.G. Falk, Geneva

Erich Goeritz, Berlin, until 1933

On loan to the Tel Aviv Museum from
Erich Goeritz, 1933–1956

Thomas Goeritz, London

Private Collection   *TAM only*

19

Statuette
(1915)
painted terra-cotta
11¾ (30) h.
signed: *Archipenko*

Provenance

From the artist

Probably S.G. Falk, Geneva

Erich Goeritz, Berlin, until 1933

On loan to the Tel Aviv Museum from
Erich Goeritz, 1933–1956

Private Collection, London

20

**Before the Mirror
(In the Boudoir)**
(1915)
oil and pencil on wood, paper, and
metal (with photograph of the artist)
18 x 12 (45.7 x 30.5)
signed: A. *Archipenko*

Provenance

Probably from the artist, c. 1924

Dr. Christian Brinton, Philadelphia

Philadelphia Museum of Art, Given by
Christian Brinton

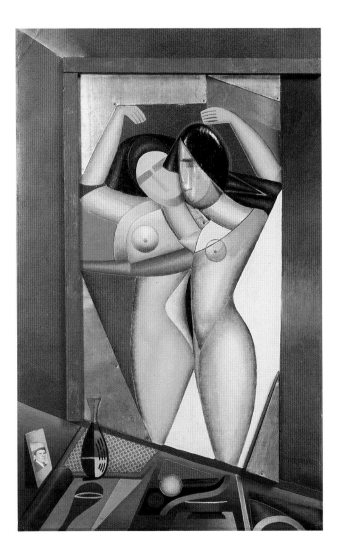

21

Woman with Fan II
1915
painted wood relief
18⅛ x 14¾ x 1 (46 x 37.5 x 2.4)
signed: *Archipenko/1915 Nice*

Provenance

From the artist

Madame Jean G. Verdier, Cannes,
France, 1921–1964

Joseph H. Hirshhorn, New York,
1964–1966

Hirshhorn Museum and Sculpture
Garden, Smithsonian Institution,
Washington

**In the Café
(Woman with Cup)**
(1915)
painted wood and painted canvas
mounted on wood
24½ x 17 x 3½ (62.3 x 43.2 x 8.8)
signed: A. *Archipenko/Nice*

Provenance

From the artist

Madame Jean G. Verdier, Cannes,
France, 1921–1964

Joseph H. Hirshhorn, New York,
1964–1966

Hirshhorn Museum and Sculpture
Garden, Smithsonian Institution,
Washington

23

Bather
1915
painted plaster on papier-mâché and
wire support
18 (45.7) h.
signed: *Archipenko/1915 Nice*

Provenance
Leonard Hutton Gallery, New York,
1973

Donald Karshan Collection, Florida

Woman at Her Toilet
(Woman before Mirror)
1916
painted wood, painted sheet metal;
support: oil on cardboard
33⅞ x 25⅜ x 2 (86 x 64.5 x 5)
signed, lower left: *Archipenko/Paris
1916*

Provenance

From the artist

S.G. Falk, Geneva

Erich Goeritz, Berlin, until 1933

On loan to the Tel Aviv Museum from
Erich Goeritz, 1933–1956

The Tel Aviv Museum, Gift of the
Goeritz Family, London, 1956

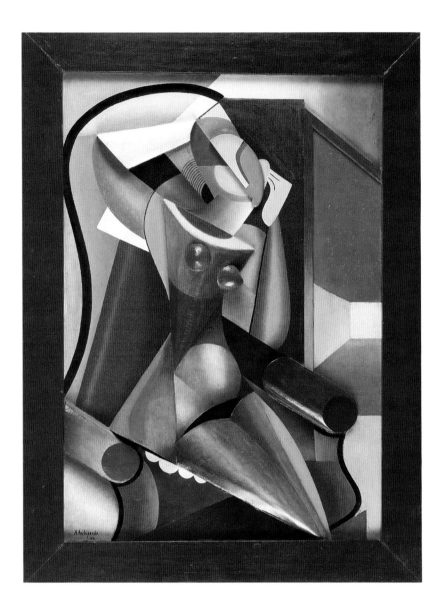

25

Kneeling Woman

(1916–1917)

painted wood; support: oil on burlap
mounted on wood

35 x 18½ x 5½ (89 x 47 x 14)

signed, lower left: *Archipenko/Nice*

Provenance

From the artist

Probably S.G. Falk, Geneva

Erich Goeritz, Berlin, until 1933

On loan to the Tel Aviv Museum from
Erich Goeritz, 1933–1956

The Tel Aviv Museum, Gift of the
Goeritz Family, London, 1956

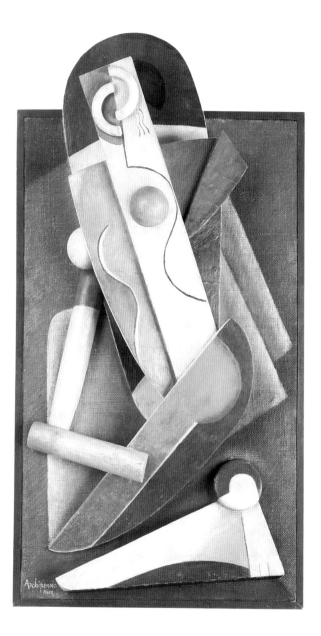

26

Woman in Room

1917

painted wood, ink drawing on paper
(collage); support: oil on wood panels
covered with gessoed oilcloth

17⅝ x 11 x 1 (45.5 x 28.3 x 2.5)

signed, lower right: A. *Archipenko*/*1917*

Provenance

From the artist

Probably S.G. Falk, Geneva

Erich Goeritz, Berlin, until 1933

On loan to the Tel Aviv Museum from
Erich Goeritz, 1933–1956

Private Collection, London

Walking Soldier
1917
painted plaster
15¾ (40) h.
signed in black paint: *Archipenko/1917*

Provenance

From the artist

S.G. Falk, Geneva

Erich Goeritz, Berlin, until 1933

On loan to the Tel Aviv Museum from
Erich Goeritz, 1933–1956

The Tel Aviv Museum, Gift of the
Goeritz Family, London, 1956

Vase Woman II
1919
bronze
22⅝ (57.5) h.
signed: *Archipenko/19*

Provenance

From the artist

Katherine S. Dreier

The Solomon R. Guggenheim
Museum, New York, Gift, Katherine
S. Dreier Estate, 1953

NGA only (illustrated)

Vase Woman II
1919
bronze
22⅝ (57) h.
signed: *Archipenko/19*

Provenance

From the artist

Probably S.G. Falk, Geneva

Erich Goeritz, Berlin, until 1933

On loan to the Tel Aviv Museum from
Erich Goeritz, 1933–1956

The Tel Aviv Museum, Gift of the
Goeritz Family, London, 1956

TAM only

29

**Seated Woman
(Geometric Figure Seated)**
(1920)
painted plaster
22½ (57) h.
signed in black paint: *Archipenko*

Provenance

From the artist

S.G. Falk, Geneva

Erich Goeritz, Berlin, until 1933

On loan to the Tel Aviv Museum from
Erich Goeritz, 1933–1956

The Tel Aviv Museum, Gift of the
Goeritz Family, London, 1956

30

**Double Portrait
(Mr. and Mrs. Falk)**
(1920)
polychromed painted plaster
29½ (75) h.
signed: *Archipenko*

Provenance

From the artist

S.G. Falk Collection, Geneva

Erich Goeritz, Berlin, until 1933

On loan to the Tel Aviv Museum from
Erich Goeritz, 1933–1956

The Tel Aviv Museum, Gift of the
Goeritz Family, London, 1956

31

Woman
(1920)
sheet metal; support: oil on burlap on
wood panel
73½ x 32¼ x 5⅛ (187 x 82 x 13)
signed, lower right: *Archipenko/Paris*

Provenance

From the artist

S.G. Falk, Geneva

Erich Goeritz, Berlin, until 1933

On loan to the Tel Aviv Museum from
Erich Goeritz, 1933–1956

The Tel Aviv Museum, Gift of the
Goeritz Family, London, 1956

32

Two Women
1920
painted wood and sheet metal
69¾ x 38¼ (177 x 97)
signed: A *Archipenko/Zurich, I.* 1920

Provenance
Ljubomir Micić, c. 1926–1971
Micić Estate, 1980

National Museum, Belgrade

33

Woman (Metal Lady)
1923
painted brass, copper, and white metal
alloy over wood core
54 x 20¾ (137 x 52.7)
with integral frame
dated: 1923; on plaque attached to
bottom edge of frame:
A. *Archipenko*

Provenance
From the artist
Katherine S. Dreier, 1924–1948

Yale University Art Gallery, Gift of
Katherine S. Dreier to the Collection
Société Anonyme

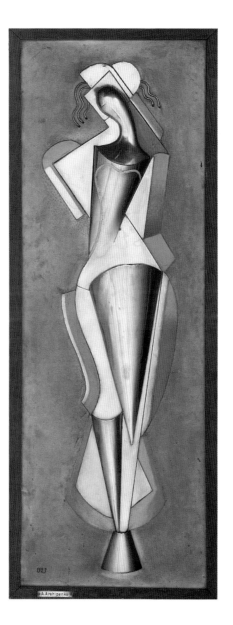

34

Standing Vertical
(1935)
painted wood
43¼ (109.8) h. with base

Frances Archipenko Gray

35

Head
(1936)
painted terra-cotta
17 (43) h.
signed: *Archipenko*

Frances Archipenko Gray

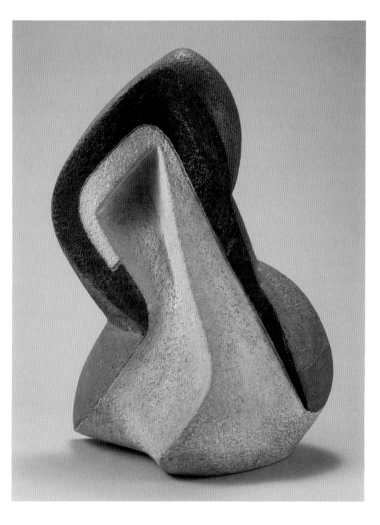

36

Walking Woman
(1937)
painted terra-cotta
25½ (65) h.
signed: *Archipenko*

Provenance

Cranbrook Academy of Art, Bloomfield
Hills, Michigan

Parke Bernet Galleries, Inc., 1972

Courtesy of Perls Galleries, New York

Spanish Woman (Espagnol)
(1942)
inlaid terra-cotta
14½ (36.8) h.
signed: *Archipenko*

Frances Archipenko Gray

Architectural Figure
(c. 1950; formerly dated 1937)
painted wood
36½ (92.7) h. with base
signed: *Archipenko*

Frances Archipenko Gray

39

Ascension
(1950)
carved plastic with illumination
38 (96.5) h. without base

Frances Archipenko Gray

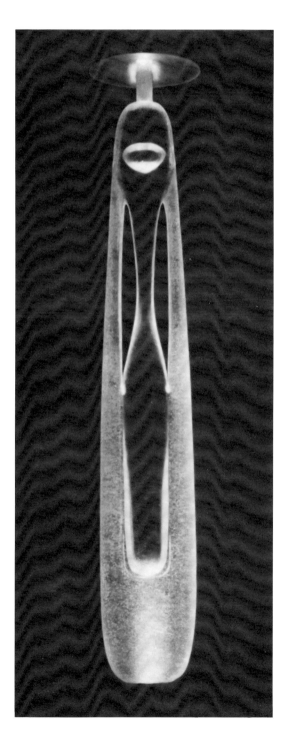

Queen
(1954)
painted wood
36½ (92.7) h. with base
signed: *Archipenko*

Frances Archipenko Gray

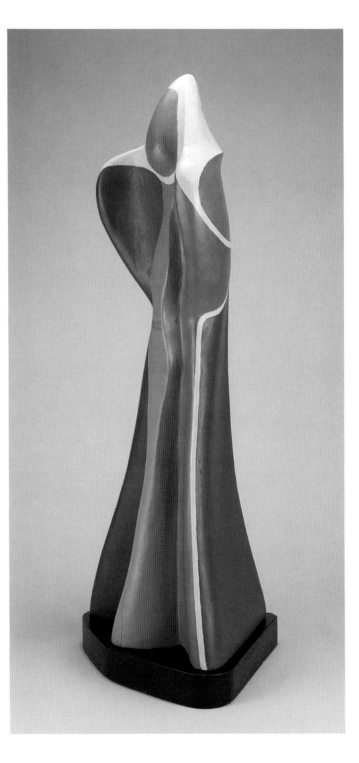

41

Figure (Fragmentary Figure)
(1957)
painted terra-cotta
19½ (49.5) h. with base

Frances Archipenko Gray

42

Cleopatra (Repose)
1957
painted wood and bakelite, found
objects
38 x 84 (96.5 x 213)
signed: *Archipenko 57*

Frances Archipenko Gray

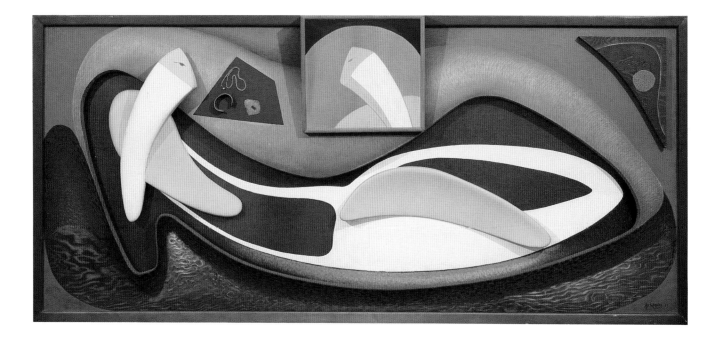

King Solomon
1963
painted hydrocal
28 (71) h. with base
signed: *Archipenko 63*

Frances Archipenko Gray

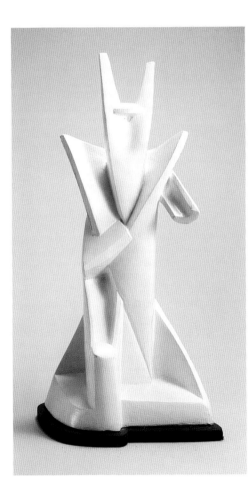

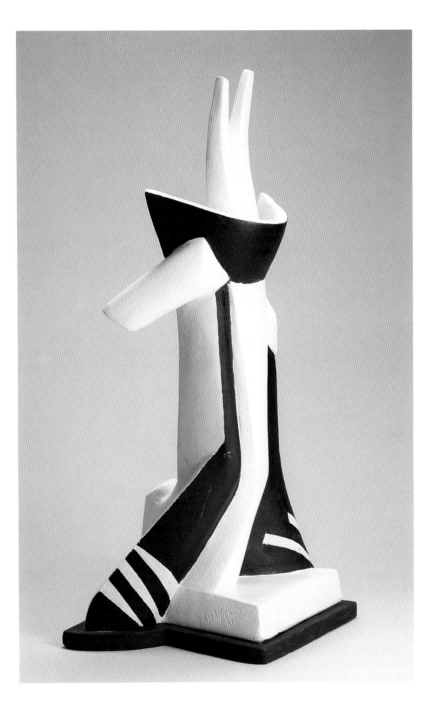

BIBLIOGRAPHY

Archipenko Exhibition Catalogues

Annandale-on-Hudson, N.Y., 1985, Edith C. Blum Institute, Bard College, *Archipenko: Drawings, Reliefs and Constructions*, Joan Marter et al. (24 August– 26 October).

Berlin, 1913, Der Sturm Gallery, *Siebzehnte Ausstellung: Alexander Archipenko*, intro. by Guillaume Apollinaire (September).

Berlin, 1921, Der Sturm Gallery, *Fünfundneunzigste Ausstellung: Alexander Archipenko* (March); exhibition traveled to Dresden, Wiesbaden, Hannover, and Munich.

Chicago, 1933, Ukrainian Pavilion, *A Century of Progress, The Archipenko Exhibition of Sculpture and Painting*, intro. by C. J. Bulliet.

Chicago, 1968, Kovler Gallery, *Archipenko: Content and Continuity, 1908–1963*, text by Donald H. Karshan and Marjorie Kovler.

Chicago, 1973, Ukrainian Institute of Modern Art, *Archipenko*, texts by Arcadia Olenska-Petryshyn and W. Kacurovsky.

Danville, Kentucky, 1985, Norton Center, Center College, *Archipenko: Sculpture, Drawings and Prints, 1908–1963*, collected, viewed, and documented by Donald H. Karshan (23 March–6 May).

Denver, 1927, *Tour of the Exhibition of the Works of Alexander Archipenko*, intro. by C. J. Bulliet; exhibition traveled to Los Angeles, San Diego, Oakland, and Portland.

Düsseldorf, 1955–1956, *Wanderausstellung: A. Archipenko, Plastik, Malerei, Zeichnungen, Druckgraphik*, intro. by Erich Wiese; exhibition traveled to Darmstadt, Mannheim, and Recklinghausen.

Düsseldorf, 1962, Galerie Wilhelm Grosshennig, *Alexander Archipenko: Plastiken aus allen Schaffensperioden.*

Frankfurt, 1922, *Kunstsalon Ludwig Schames, Alexander Archipenko, Elfte retrospektive Ausstellung. Lyonel Feininger*, texts by Archipenko and Wilhelm Hausenstein (May).

Geneva, 1919, Librarie Kundig, *Tournée de l'Exposition de Sculptures, Sculpto-Peintures, Peintures, Dessins de Alexandre Archipenko*, preface by Maurice Raynal (24 November–10 December); Zürich, 1920, Kunsthaus (8 January–8 February).

Guatemala City, 1953, El Instituto Guatemalteco-Americano, *Una Exposicion de Dibujos del Escultor Norteamericano Alexander Archipenko.*

Hagen, 1912, Folkwang Museum, *Le Fauconnier. Alexander Archipenko*, intro. by Guillaume Apollinaire (7 December 1912–8 January 1913).

Hagen, 1960, Karl-Ernst Osthaus Museum, *Alexander Archipenko: Plastiken, 1909–1959*, intro. by Erich Wiese; exhibition traveled to Münster, Saarbrücken, and Düsseldorf.

Hollywood, California, 1929, 1931, Braxton Gallery, *The Archipenko Exhibition*, intro. by Harry Braxton.

Los Angeles, 1967, UCLA Art Galleries, *Alexander Archipenko* (traveling exhibition to ten U.S. museums), texts by Katharine Kuh, Frances Archipenko, Frederick S. Wight, and Donald H. Karshan.

Milan, 1963, Centro Culturale S. Fedele, *Mostra Antologica di Archipenko*, intro. by Giovanni Cappelletto.

Munich, 1964, Galerie Stangl, *Alexander Archipenko: Ausstellung mit Skulpturen und Zeichnungen* (14 February–4 April).

New York, 1921, Société Anonyme, Inc., *Archipenko*, text by Iwan Goll (trans. from French by Mary Knoblauch) (1 February–15 March).

New York, 1924, Kingore Gallery, under the auspices of the Société Anonyme, *The Archipenko Exhibition*, intro. and catalogue by Christian Brinton (20 January–4 February).

New York, 1928, The Anderson Galleries, *Archipenko, Catalogue of Exhibition and Description of Archipentura* (October).

New York, 1932, John Levy Galleries, *A. Archipenko. Exhibition of New Works.*

New York, 1944, Nierendorf Gallery, *Alexander Archipenko, Works from 1909–1944* (18 January– 5 February).

New York, 1954, Associated American Artists Galleries, *Archipenko, 110th Exhibition, Fifty Years Production*, intro. by Alexander Archipenko (16 October– 14 November).

New York, 1957, Perls Galleries, *Archipenko: Recent Polychromes* (14 October–9 November).

New York, 1959, Perls Galleries, *Alexander Archipenko: Bronzes* (29 September–24 October).

New York, 1962, Perls Galleries, *Alexander Archipenko Bronzes* (9 January–3 February).

New York, 1970, The Museum of Modern Art, *Archipenko: The Parisian Years*, intros. by William S. Lieberman and Katharine Kuh (20 July–18 October).

New York, 1970, Bernard Danenberg Galleries, Inc., *Archipenko, The American Years, 1923–1963*, intro. by Frederick S. Wight (23 July–15 August).

New York, 1973, The Pace Gallery, *Archipenko at Pace* (22 September–20 October).

New York, 1976, Zabriskie Gallery, *Archipenko: Polychrome Sculptures*, intro. by Katherine Jánszky Michaelsen (27 October–20 November); Chicago, 1977, Arts Club (10 January–11 February).

New York, 1979, Zabriskie Gallery, *Alexander Archipenko (1887–1964): The Late Experimental Years* (2 October–27 October).

New York, 1982, Zabriskie Gallery, *Archipenko, Naturalism of the Twenties and Thirties* (17 March–17 April).

Omaha, 1939, University of Omaha, *Alexander Archipenko in Retrospect* (29 October–10 December).

Omaha, 1949, University of Omaha, *Alexander Archipenko* (4 March–25 March).

Potsdam, 1921, Gustav Kiepenheuer Verlag, *Alexander Archipenko, Retrospektive Ausstellung*, intro. by Iwan Goll.

Prague, 1923, Publicace Devetsilu, *Archipenko*, text by Karel Teige (April–May).

Rome, 1963, Ente Premi Roma, *Archipenko*, intros. by Giovanni Sangiorgi and Jacopo Recupero.

São Paulo, Brazil, 1952, Museu de Arte Moderna de São Paulo, *Desenhos de Archipenko*, intro. by Wolfgang Pfeiffer (November).

St. Gallen, Switzerland, 1962, Galerie "Im Erker," *Alexander Archipenko*, intro. by Werner Hofmann (17 November–10 January 1963).

Tel Aviv, 1981, The Tel Aviv Museum, *Archipenko, The Early Works: 1910–1921*, texts by Donald H. Karshan, Edna Moshenson, and Marc Scheps (April–September).

Tokyo, 1974, Fuji Television Gallery, *Alexander Archipenko* (5 April–24 April).

Venice, 1920, XIIa Esposizione Internazionale d'Arte della Città di Venezia, *Mostra Individuale di Alexandre Archipenko* (15 April–31 October).

Washington, D.C., 1969, National Collection of Fine Arts, *Archipenko: International Visionary* (a retrospective traveling exhibition organized by the International Art Program, Smithsonian Institution), ed. Donald H. Karshan.

Winnipeg, Canada, 1962, Winnipeg Art Gallery, *Archipenko*, intro. by Ferdinand Eckhardt.

Works about Archipenko

Apollinaire, Guillaume, "Alexandre Archipenko." *Der Sturm*, Jahrg. IV, Heft 200 (1913), 194.

Archipenko, Alexander, "Nature, The Point of Departure." *The Arts*, vol. V, no. 1 (January 1924), 32.

Archipenko, Alexander, and Fifty Art Historians. *Archipenko, Fifty Creative Years, 1908–1958*. New York, 1960.

Alexander Archipenko, Sturm Bilderbücher II. Berlin, 1917.

Alexander Archipenko Papers. Archives of American Art, Smithsonian Institution, Washington.

Barbantini, Nino. "1920. Cézanne. Archipenko." *Biennali* (1945), 39–40, 48–54.

Däubler, Theodor, and Iwan Goll (with poem by Blaise Cendrars). *Archipenko Album*. Potsdam, 1921.

Dreier, Katherine S. "Alexander Archipenko at Anderson Galleries." *Brochure Quarterly* (October 1928–January 1929), 20–21.

Geist, Sidney. Review of *Archipenko, Fifty Creative Years, 1908–1958*, by Alexander Archipenko. *Arts Magazine* (September 1961), 71–72.

Goll, Iwan. "Archipenko." *Action* 5 (October 1920), 58–60.

Goll, Iwan. "Archipenko." *Horizont* 26 (1921), n.p.

Goll, Iwan. "Archipenko." *Ma—Aktivista Folyóirat* VI, no. 6 (25 April 1921), 71–78.

Habasque, Guy. "Archipenko." *L'Oeil* 78 (June 1961), 38–45.

Halle, Fannina W. "Kandinsky, Archipenko, Chagall." *Die Bildenden Künste*, Jahrg. IV, Heft 11/12 (1921), 177–187.

Hildebrandt, Hans. *Alexander Archipenko*. Berlin, 1923 (editions in English, French, Spanish, and Ukrainian).

Huszár, Vilmos. "Alexander Archipenko." *de Stijl*, no. 2 (January 1917).

Karshan, Donald H. "Alexander Archipenko—in Retrospect." *Journal of the Archives of American Art* 7, no. 2 (April 1967), 4–15.

Karshan, Donald H. "American Printmaking, 1670–1968." *Art in America* 56, no. 4 (1968), 22–55.

Karshan, Donald H. "Archipenko." *Arts Magazine* 42, no. 6 (April 1968), 36–38.

Karshan, Donald H. *Archipenko, The Sculpture and Graphic Art*. Tübingen, 1974.

Karshan, Donald H. "The Graphics of Archipenko." *Artists Proof*, VII (1967), 72–77.

Karshan, Donald H. "Les revolutions d'Alexandre Archipenko." *Plaisir de France*, no. 421 (July 1974).

Kramer, Hilton. "A Chance to Re-Evaluate Archipenko's Stature." *The New York Times* (24 July 1970).

Kramer, Hilton. "The Two Archipenkos." *The New York Times* (2 August 1970).

Michaelsen, Katherine Jánszky. *Archipenko, A Study of the Early Works, 1908–1920*. PhD. diss., Columbia

University, 1975. New York, 1977.

Michaelsen, Katherine Jánszky. "The Chronology of Archipenko's Paris Years." *Arts Magazine* (November 1976), 91–93.

Mitzitch (Micić), Lioubomir. *Archipenko, Plastique Nouvelle.* Belgrade, 1923.

Raynal, Maurice. *A. Archipenko.* Rome, 1923.

Raynal, Maurice. "Alexandre Archipenko." *Der Ararat* 2 (1921), 183–194.

Raynal, Maurice. "Die Skulptomalerei." *Der Ararat* 5/6 (March 1920), 33–34.

Rzepecki, Nestor. "Archipenko Interview." *Pace,* vol. II, no. 3 (June 1955), 10–17.

Sangiorgi, Giovanni. "La Pittura Scultorea di Archipenko." *Civiltà della Macchina* 5 (September–October 1963), 35–42.

Schacht, Roland. "Archipenko, Belling und Westheim." *Der Sturm,* Jahrg. 40, Heft 5 (May 1923), 76–78.

Schacht, Roland. *Alexander Archipenko. Sturm Bilderbücher II.* Berlin, 1924 (expanded).

Subotić, Irina. "Une Nouvelle Acquisition du Musée National de Belgrade: *Deux Femmes* d'Alexandre Archipenko. Archipenko en Yougoslavie." *Recueil du Musée National,* XI-2 Histoire de l'art (Belgrade, 1982), 209–233.

Taillandier, Yvon. "Conversation avec Archipenko." *XX Siècle,* n.s., XXV année, no. 22 (Christmas 1963).

Wiese, Erich. "Alexander Archipenko." *Junge Kunst,* Band 40 (1923).

Selected Books and Periodicals

Alloway, Lawrence. *The Venice Biennale, 1895–1968. From Salon to Goldfishbowl.* London, 1968.

Andersen, Wayne. *American Sculpture in Process: 1930/ 1970.* Boston, 1975.

L'Année 1913. Les formes ethétiques de l'oeuvre d'art à la veille de la première guerre mondiale. Ed. Lilliane Brion-Guerry, 2 vols. Paris, 1971.

Apollinaire on Art, Essays and Reviews, 1902–1918. Ed. LeRoy C. Breunig, trans. Susan Suleiman. New York, 1972.

Archivi del Futurismo. Eds. Maria Drudi Gambillo and Teresa Fiori, 2 vols. Rome, 1958–1962.

Armstrong, Tom, et al. *200 Years of American Sculpture.* Whitney Museum of American Art, New York, 1976.

Barnett, Vivian Endicott. *Handbook. The Guggenheim Museum Collection, 1900–1980.* The Solomon R. Guggenheim Museum, New York, 1984.

Barr, Alfred H., Jr. *Cubism and Abstract Art.* The Museum of Modern Art, New York, 1936.

Barron, Stefanie. *German Expressionist Sculpture.* Los Angeles County Museum of Art, Los Angeles, 1984.

Basler, Adolphe. *La sculpture moderne en France.* Paris, 1920.

The Blue Four: Feininger, Jawlensky, Kandinsky, Paul Klee. Foreword by Peg Weiss. Leonard Hutton Galleries, New York, 1984.

Brown, Milton W. *American Painting from the Armory Show to the Depression.* Princeton, N.J., 1970.

Burnham, Jack. *Beyond Modern Sculpture. The Effects of Science and Technology on the Sculpture of this Century.* New York, 1968.

Cachin, Françoise. "Futurism in Paris, 1909–1913." *Art in America* (March–April 1974), 39–44.

Casson, Stanley. *XXc. Sculptors.* London, 1930.

Chapiro, Jacques. *La Ruche.* Paris, 1960.

Cooper, Douglas. *The Cubist Epoch.* New York, 1971.

Descargues, Pierre. *Fernand Léger.* Paris, 1955.

Dorival, Bernard. "Les omissions d'Archipenko et Lipchitz." *Bulletin de la societé de l'histoire de l'art français* (1974), 201–220.

Dorival, Bernard. *Les peintres du vingtième siècle.* Paris, 1957.

Dresdener Sezession, 1919–1923. Intros. by Fritz Löffler and Joachim Heusinger von Waldegg. Galleria del Levante, Munich, 1977.

Einstein, Carl. *Die Kunst des 20. Jahrhunderts.* Berlin, 1926.

Elsen, Albert E. *Origins of Modern Sculpture: Pioneers and Premises.* New York, 1974.

Elsen, Albert E. *The Partial Figure in Modern Sculpture.* Baltimore Museum of Art, Baltimore, 1969.

Ferenczy, Béni. *Irás és Kép.* Budapest, 1961.

Fry, Edward. *Cubism.* New York, 1966.

Golding, John. *Cubism: A History and an Analysis, 1907–1914.* New York, 1968 (rev. ed.).

Golding, John, and Christopher Green. *Léger and Purist Paris.* The Tate Gallery, London, 1971.

Gordon, Donald R. *Modern Art Exhibitions, 1900–1916.* Munich, 1974.

Gray, Christopher. *Cubist Aesthetic Theories.* Baltimore, 1953.

Hamilton, George Heard. *Painting and Sculpture in Europe, 1880–1940.* Baltimore, 1983 (rev. ed.).

Hamilton, George Heard, and William C. Agee. *Raymond Duchamp-Villon, 1879–1918.* New York, 1967.

Hammacher, A. M. *Jacques Lipchitz.* trans. James Brockway. New York, 1975.

Henderson, Linda Dalrymple. *The Fourth Dimension and Non-Euclidian Geometry in Modern Art.* Princeton, N.J., 1983.

Hildebrandt, Hans. *Die Kunst des XIX und XX Jahrhunderts.* Potsdam, 1924.

Hofmann, Werner. *The Sculpture of Henri Laurens.* New York, 1970.

Kuhn, Alfred. *Die Neuere Plastik.* Munich, 1921.

Lipchitz, Jacques, and H. H. Arnason, *My Life in Sculpture.* New York, 1972.

Martin, Marianne W. *Futurist Art and Theory, 1909–1915.* London, 1968.

McCabe, Cynthia Jafee. *The Golden Door, Artist-Immigrants of America, 1876–1976.* Hirshhorn Museum and Sculpture Garden, Smithsonian Institution, Washington, 1976.

Michaelsen, Katherine Jánszky. "Early Mixed-Media Constructions." *Arts Magazine* (January 1976), 72–76.

Michaelsen, Katherine Jánszky. Review of *The Planar Dimension, Europe, 1912–1932,* by Margit Rowell. The Solomon R. Guggenheim Museum, New York, *The Structurist* 19/20 (1979–1980), 125–131.

Milner, John. *Vladimir Tatlin and the Russian Avant-Garde.* New Haven and London, 1983.

Moholy-Nagy, László. *The New Vision and Abstract of an Artist.* New York, 1946.

Moholy-Nagy, László. *Vision in Motion.* Chicago, 1946.

Moholy-Nagy, Sibyl. *Moholy-Nagy, Experiment in Totality.* New York, 1950.

The Museum of Modern Art Archives: Alfred Barr Papers. Archives of American Art, Smithsonian Institution, Washington.

Nash, Steven A., and Jörn Merkert. *Naum Gabo, Sixty Years of Constructivism.* Dallas Museum of Art, Dallas and Munich, 1985.

Olson, Ruth, and Abraham Chanin. *Gabo-Pevsner.* New York, 1948.

Karl-Ernst Osthaus, Leben und Werk. Recklinghausen, 1971.

Paris-Berlin, 1900–1933. Centre national d'art et de culture Georges Pompidou, Paris, 1978.

Passuth, Krisztina. *László Moholy-Nagy.* New York, 1985.

Rickey, George. *Constructivism, Origins and Evolution.* New York, 1967.

Roh, Franz. *"Entartete Kunst," Kunst-Barbarei im Dritten Reich.* Hannover, 1962.

Rosenblum, Robert. *Cubism and Twentieth Century Art.* New York, 1966 (rev. ed.).

Vladimir Baranoff-Rossiné. Musée national d'art moderne, Paris, 1973.

Rowell, Margit. *The Planar Dimension: Europe, 1912–1932.* The Solomon R. Guggenheim Museum, New York, 1979.

Rudenstine, Angelica Zander. *Peggy Guggenheim Collection, Venice.* New York, 1985.

Russian Avant-Garde, 1908–1922. Leonard Hutton Galleries, New York, 1971.

Sammlung Walden: Gemälde, Zeichnungen, Plastiken. Achtes Verzeichnis. Berlin (October 1919).

Sapori, Francesco. *La dodicesima esposizione d'arte a Venezia.* Bergamo, 1920.

Galka Scheyer Papers, Archives of American Art, Smithsonian Institution, Washington.

Severini, Gino. *Tutta la vita di un pittore.* Milan, 1946.

The Société Anonyme Collection, Collection of American Literature. Beinecke Rare Book and Manuscript Library, Yale University.

The Société Anonyme and the Dreier Bequest at Yale University. A Catalogue Raisonné. Eds. Robert L. Herbert, Eleanor S. Apter, and Elise K. Kenney. New Haven and London, 1984.

Soffici, Ardengo. *Trinta artisti moderni italiani e stranieri.* Florence, 1950.

Soffici, Ardengo. *Memoirs.* 2 vols. Florence, 1968.

Steneberg, Eberhard. *Russische Kunst: Berlin, 1919–1932.* Berlin, 1969.

Subotić, Irina. "Die Zeitschrift 'Zenit' und die Erscheinung des Konstruktivismus." *Jugoslawischer Konstruktivismus, 1921–1981.* Stadmuseum Ratigen, 1981.

Umanskij, Konstantin. *Neue Kunst in Russland, 1914–1919.* Potsdam, 1920.

Walden, Herwarth. *Einblick in Kunst: Expressionismus, Futurismus, Kubismus.* Berlin, 1924.

Walden, Nell, and Lothar Schreyer. *Der Sturm: Ein Erinnerungsbuch an Herwarth Walden und die Künstler aus dem Sturm Kreis.* Baden-Baden, 1954.

Wasserman, Jeanne L. *Three American Sculptors and the Female Nude: Lachaise, Nadelman, Archipenko.* Fogg Art Museum, Cambridge, 1980.

Wescher, Herta. *Die Collage: Geschichte eines künstlerisches Ausdruckmittels.* Cologne, 1968.

Westheim, Paul. *Architecktonik des Plastischen.* Berlin, 1923.

Willrich, Wolfgang. *Säuberung des Kunsttempels.* Munich and Berlin, 1939.

Wingler, Hans M. *The Bauhaus, Weimar, Dessau, Berlin, Chicago.* Cambridge, Mass. and London, 1978.

PHOTO CREDITS

Michaelsen

Alexander Archipenko Papers, Archives of American Art, Smithsonian Institution, Washington
  Figs. 23, 30, 36a–b (Photo by Worsinger), 38a–b, 41
Art, Prints and Photographs Division, The New York Public Library, Astor, Lenox and Tilden Foundations
  Fig. 25
Courtesy of Frances Archipenko Gray, New York
  Figs. 2, 3, 5, 11, 12, 24, 27, 28, 32, 34a-b, 35
Courtesy of Katherine J. Michaelsen
  Fig. 21
Courtesy of The Tel Aviv Museum
  Fig. 29 (Photo by Avraham Hay)
Courtesy of Zabriskie Gallery
  Figs. 16 (Photo by Geoffrey Clements, New York), 33, 37, 40
Photo by Dölf Preisig, Zürich
  Fig. 1
Landesbildstelle Niederrhein, Düsseldorf
  Fig. 39
Photo by Eric E. Mitchell
  Fig. 19
Photo by Joseph Szaszfai
  Fig. 22

Guralnik

Avraham Hay, Tel Aviv
  Figs. 18, 22, 24, 26-30
Courtesy of Manfred Lehmbruck
  Fig. 12
Courtesy of the Staatsgalerie, Stuttgart
  Fig. 15, 16 (© Karl-Heinrich Müller Insel Hombroich, Neuss)
Foto Soprintendenza Archeologica di Roma
  Fig. 19
Photo by Ran Erde, Tel Aviv
  Fig. 23
Photo by Judy and Kenny, Tel Aviv
  Fig. 25
Réunion des musées nationaux, Paris
  Figs. 19-21
The Tel Aviv Museum Archives
  Figs. 1, 2 (Photo by Abraham Soskin), 3–5, 6 (Photo by I. Zafrir), 7-11 (Photos by Avraham Hay)

Catalogue illustrations

Photos by:
David Allison
  Cat. nos. 34, 35, 37, 38, 40, 41, 43
Prudence Cuming Associates Limited
  Cat. no. 19
Rolf Giesen
  Cat. no. 3
Avraham Hay
  Cat. nos. 4, 12, 13, 15, 17, 27, 30, 31
Judy and Kenny
  Cat. nos. 5, 24, 29
Robert E. Mates
  Cat. nos. 14, 28
Eric E. Mitchell
  Cat. no. 20
Valdimir Popović, Belgrade
  Cat. no. 32
Lee Stalsworth
  Cat. nos. 1, 21
Joseph Szaszfai
  Cat. no. 33
John Tennant
  Cat. no. 22